Charles Best Robinson

New South Wales

The Oldest and Richest of the Australian Colonies

Charles Best Robinson

New South Wales
The Oldest and Richest of the Australian Colonies

ISBN/EAN: 9783337004620

Printed in Europe, USA, Canada, Australia, Japan

Cover: Foto ©ninafisch / pixelio.de

More available books at **www.hansebooks.com**

NEW SOUTH WALES.

CONTENTS.

	Page.
I.—INTRODUCTION	1
II.—POLITICAL CONSTITUTION	6
III.—AGRICULTURAL SETTLEMENT—	
How to get Land	9
Pioneer Work	10
The Settler's Home	12
The Farmer's Prospects	12
Productions of the Soil—	
Wheat	14
Maize and Maizena	17
Sugar: Growth and Manufacture	17
The Vine: Wine-making	20
Tobacco: Growth and Manufacture	21
Cereal and other Crops	22
Semi-tropical Productions	23
Dried Fruits	23
Vegetable Fibres, &c.	24
Sericulture	24
Fruits, &c.	25
Occupation of Soil	27
Waste Lands	27
Agricultural Produce: Supply and Demand	28
Balance of Imports over Exports—1871	28
IV.—PASTORAL OCCUPATION—	
Character and Extent	28
Sheep	30
Horned Cattle	30
Horses, Pigs, &c.	31
Preserved Meats	31
Pastoral Progress	32

CONTENTS.

	Page.
V.—MINERAL WEALTH—	
Gold Discovery	34
Gold in the Soil	35
Gold in the Rock	36
The Miner in New South Wales	42
Gold Production and Prospects	46
Coal	49
Kerosene	52
Iron	53
Copper	55
Tin	56
Silver, Lead, Cinnabar, Diamonds, &c.	61
Mineral Lands: how obtained	62
VI.—MANUFACTURING INDUSTRIES—	
Iron Trades	63
Smelting Works	65
Ship and House Building: Indigenous Timbers	66
Coach and Carriage Trades	67
Stone and Earth	68
Leather, &c.	68
Woollen Cloths	68
Manufactures in New South Wales	69
VII.—REVENUE: BANKS, &c.	70
VIII.—TRADE	72
IX.—HARBOURS AND RIVERS	76
X.—FISHERIES	78
XI.—THE PORT AND CITY OF SYDNEY	79
XII.—RAILWAYS, ROADS, AND TELEGRAPHS	82
XIII.—POSTAL ARRANGEMENTS: MONEY ORDERS: GOVERNMENT SAVINGS BANKS	84, 85
XIV.—LABOUR AND WAGES	86
XV.—COST OF LIVING—	
Food and Rent	87
Provisions and Clothing	90
XVI.—EDUCATION, LITERATURE, AND RELIGION	90
XVII.—SOCIAL CONDITION OF THE PEOPLE	94
A Public Holiday in Sydney	98

CONTENTS.

	Page.
XVIII.—HINTS TO EMIGRANTS	101
XIX.—SUMMARY OF THE ADVANTAGES OF NEW SOUTH WALES AS A HOME FOR THE IMMIGRANT	103
XX.—APPENDIX—	
List of Gold Fields in New South Wales, and Area of each	105
Governor; Ministry	106
Population; Births, &c.; Schools, &c.	106
Land Sales; Acres under Crop; Live Stock, &c.	107
Mills and Manufactories; Coal; Shipping	108
Total Imports and Exports, &c.	108
Telegrams; Money Orders; Postal; Revenue; Expenditure, &c.	109
Exports:—Wool; Leather; Tallow; Gold; Coal; Timber	110

NEW SOUTH WALES.

I.—INTRODUCTION.

THE Australasian Colonies are rapidly becoming the most important of all the dependencies of the British Crown. It is only 103 years since Captain Cook planted the British flag on these distant and unknown shores, and only 85 years since England discovered the vast resources which Providence had here entrusted to her care, and recognized the possibility of establishing in New South Wales another branch of her industrious and enterprising people. Now there is already settled on these lands an English-speaking population of over 2,000,000, self-governing and self-dependent, but proud of their common ancestry, faithful in their allegiance to the Mother Country, and developing a trade with her which is increasing year by year with almost unparalleled rapidity.

Of these Colonies New South Wales claims to be the oldest, the most extensively settled, the most varied in soil and climate, and the most richly endowed by Nature with all sources of agricultural, pastoral and mineral wealth. Though two independent Colonies have been successively detached from it—Victoria on the south-west, and Queensland on the north—New South Wales still embraces a magnificent territory of 323,437 square miles, stretching in a south-westerly direction from 28° 10′ south to 37° 28′ south, and sweeping westward for 800 miles from the Pacific seaboard to the vast central plains of the continent: an area equal to that of France, Great Britain and Ireland combined, and larger than any European State with the single exception of Russia. The whole of this territory lies beyond the tropics, within the most favoured belt of the globe; and instead of being the barren sandy desert which early explorers imagined, comprises some of the most valuable agricultural areas and some of the richest and most extensive natural pasture lands to be found in the World. The physical aspect of the Colony is very marked, and

B

may be easily described. Through its entire length a mountain range stretches from north to south, throwing out spurs to the east and west, but in the main running parallel with the coast, at distances varying from about 25 to 120 miles. This range, known in its southern portion as the Australian Alps, and further north as the Blue Mountains, widens out at intervals into rough table-lands of 20 or 30 miles extent, with lofty peaks varying in height from 3,000 to over 7,000 feet, abounding with the wildest and most picturesque scenery, and forming the watershed of the continent, from which innumerable tributaries supply the rivers which drain the western interior on that side and flow into the Pacific Ocean on the east. This mountain tract is for the most part sterile and unproductive to the agriculturist, long a terror to the early settlers, by whom it was deemed impassable, but it makes ample amends by the inexhaustible treasures of gold, copper, tin, iron, coal and oil to be found in its offshoots and at its foot in all directions. Beyond this range there is a gradual slope to the vast plains of the interior, where millions of sheep and cattle roam at large, and enrich the enterprising settler with their produce, fed on the natural grasses alone. The narrow strip lying between the dividing range and the coast is the oldest settled and the most populous, intersected with many small rivers, undulating with hill and valley, in some places well wooded, and at intervals presenting whole districts of the richest soil adapted for all kinds of agriculture. There towns and villages are to be met with every few miles, and pretty villas, country seats and homesteads peep through the forest or nestle in the meadows on all sides. The coast line measures over 800 miles, broken with many bold headlands and indented with numerous bays, mostly narrow at the entrance, some of them leading to noble rivers impeded with sand-bars but capable of being easily cleared, and affording ports and harbours of refuge in stress of weather. The capital of the Colony, Sydney, stands at the head of Port Jackson, a harbour of romantic beauty and surpassing loveliness, wooded to the water's edge, but broken at intervals with frowning cliffs that rise to the height of 300 feet, and stretching inland in a hundred finely-rounded bays, presenting every variety of form, and fringed with wreaths of white foam all along the lines of glittering sand. Here land-locked and perfectly secure, all the mercantile and armed fleets of all nations may ride at anchor at one time, and leave space enough for the increase of hundreds of years.

Five miles from the main entrance to this magnificent natural dock the city is built, with its long streets, handsome buildings, tall masts adorned with flags of all nations, long lines of shipping and crowded warehouses, the emporium of an immense and wealthy Country, the centre of a trade with England, China, India, America, and all the Southern Isles, fast growing into colossal proportions, and proud of her title "The Queen of the Pacific." Here, on the 26th January, 1788, the first Governor, Captain Phillip, landed with his rough colonist band of 1,030 people, and his scanty supply of 431 head of cattle, poultry and other live stock all told. In 1851 the southern portion was formed into the separate Colony of Victoria, taking 68,335 of the population, and 6,026,237 head of sheep and cattle. In 1859 the northern portion was separated to form the Colony of Queensland, taking 25,000 of the population and 2,419,091 sheep; yet, on the 2nd of April, 1871, the population of New South Wales was 503,981, equal to one-fortieth of the population of England. The number of cattle was 2,014,888, and of sheep 16,278,697, equal to three-fourths of the whole stock of cattle and sheep in England. A capital has been built, with a population, including its suburbs, of over 140,000; not less than 623 post towns have been founded, some of them approaching the magnitude of cities, and one at a distance of 944 miles from Sydney; 6,114 miles of telegraph have been opened, 10,000 miles of roads have been made, 400 miles of railway have been constructed, and 300 miles more are being surveyed; one line ascending the Blue Mountains to a height of nearly 4,000 feet, and descending by means of works the most massive and ingenious; immense mines have been opened for the precious metals, and for copper, coal, tin, and other minerals. Her ports have been furnished with commodious docks and wharfs, and possess 75,224 tons of shipping, while the gross revenue of the Colony for 1872 was £4,775,540. The total export and import trade of the Colony for 1871 (the latest year for which Customs Returns have been compiled) was £20,854,540. The progress indicated by these facts is all the more valuable because it has been gradual—not the result of any sudden and extraordinary influx of population arising from exceptional circumstances. The mineral resources of the Colony, valuable as they have proved, are only just beginning to be developed; the production of gold for last year surpass anything that has been known since 1862; the deposits of copper and tin are enormous; the latter, a perfectly new industry, capable of development to any extent by the judicious application of labour and capital; while the Coal Fields are being rapidly opened for the supply of all the Australian Colonies and foreign ports, and furnish the motive power for manufacturing enterprise in future ages as extensive as that of the Mother Country. Already there are nearly 7,000 factories and workshops in full operation, including seven woollen, cloth, and tweed factories; and with the power of producing wool, cotton, silk, coal, and iron, to any extent within her borders, New South Wales is clearly marked out as the future emporium of the trade and commerce of the Pacific. The climate of the Colony is most genial, and highly favourable to health; every variety of temperature is to be found within so vast an area, and with such varied physical features. On the tablelands, frost, snow, and hail are common; on the inland plains the thermometer is over 100° in the shade for the greater part of the summer; and there are occasional droughts at the very time that part of the coast districts may be flooded; but in Sydney, which is central, the mean temperature is only 62' 4°, similar to that of Lisbon, the extreme range in the shade being 106° in summer and 36° in winter, while in London the range is from 97° to 5°. On the whole there are few parts of the Colony where the heat is more trying than the hot summer months of England; while nowhere, except at a few places on the summit of the mountain ranges, is there anything of the rigorous English winter. The air is clear and bracing, the light gorgeous, the sky, for an average of 200 days in the year, cloudless, the nights most enjoyable, with bright constellations of stars well defined, spread over the whole heavens, and the moon, when full, giving light enough to read by, and revealing the whole landscape beneath. Small-pox and many ailments of children and infectious diseases as native to the Country are quite unknown, and some that have been imported quickly die out. Even with the unsettled life incident to a new Country, its vital statistics compare favourably with those of almost any other part of the World, and give a far higher average of life than those of the United Kingdom. In no part of the British Empire are life and property more secure. Even in the mining districts, where a rush of 10,000 persons occasionally takes place in a few weeks, there is less crime and disorder than in most English towns of the same number of inhabitants. The whole Country is divided into Police Districts, and in the far interior whatever crime may be committed seldom escapes detection and punishment. The aborigines, a harmless and well-disposed race, have unfortunately almost entirely disappeared. No coloured labour is imported or employed in New South Wales. There are a few thousand Chinese in the Colony, but they are good citizens and most frugal industrious workmen. More than half the population is native-born, of the true English type, more so probably than in any other Colony. National animosities, such as cause so much disorder in the United States, scarcely exist here. Secure in the enjoyment of political and religious equality, all classes are order-loving and law-abiding; political and religious differences never lead to a breach of the peace, not even during the most excited Parliamentary and Municipal elections. Public schools are established in every part of the Colony, built partly by local subscription and partly by Parliamentary grant, and supported and controlled by the State; and these schools are highly efficient, and available for all classes of the community. Three-fourths of the population are settled in cities and towns, where all the comforts and luxuries of English life are common to every home, and few of the pastoral population are beyond a day's ride from some centre where supplies of all kinds may be obtained at reasonable prices. Wages are high, and work plentiful, and in the present revival of mining, labour is becoming still dearer and more scarce; and though in the capital there are always a few loafers lounging about the streets seeking to live by their wits at the expense of the credulous, yet no man or woman who is willing and able to work need ever be out of employment; and it has been stated in evidence before a Parliamentary Commission, that the Colony can easily absorb in all its various industries from 30,000 to 50,000 immigrants every year.

Such are some of the resources which New South Wales offers to all the industrious and enterprising of other lands, whose necessities or inclinations may induce them to seek a home beyond the seas. She has 207,000,000 acres of land, of which, at the close of 1871, only 11,000,000 were alienated, 5,000,000 being disposed of to agriculturists, and 3,000,000 leased for agricultural purposes, while 140,000,000 acres are occupied as pastoral leases, feeding 18,000,000 sheep, thus showing the value of these lands; and the whole of the area, together with the remaining 60,000,000 acres at present unoccupied, is open for the settler to select from where he chooses, on the easiest and most accommodating terms. Why should the labourer, the artisan, the small capitalist, toil through a weary life in the overcrowded labour markets of the World, in dread of pauperism and want all their days, when under the same Crown, the same laws, and among a people of the same race and language, they may find a ready welcome, full employment, liberal wages, large profits, and every facility for acquiring land and possessing homes of their own? Every immigrant is wealth to the Colony and wealth to England too, for her trade with her 2,000,000 Australian children ranks next in value to her trade with the 200,000,000 of India. We promise to no one immunity from toil. The lazy, the improvident, the drunkard, the loafer,—such as abound in all large cities and are a burden upon the community where they dwell,—these can find a Paradise nowhere, and least of all in a young Country; but honest labour of all kinds, and capital in large or small sums, seeking investment,—these may come with a certainty of a comfortable livelihood, a competence for life by a few years industry and prudence, and in many cases moderate fortune too. To all such we submit the following pages, which may be relied upon as giving a truthful account of New South Wales in its present condition, and as a field for the immigrant of every land.

II.—POLITICAL CONSTITUTION.

It is of great importance for emigrants to know the nature of the Government and political condition of the Country where they intend to settle. A despotic Government and a servile people never can prosper, and it is perhaps for these reasons that the greatest part of the magnificent lands of South America remain unoccupied. Where taxes can be arbitrarily imposed by those who govern, and where exactions can be made upon the cultivators of the soil for any amount of the produce of their labour by simple edict of the rulers, production is sure to be small and industrial progress is impossible, for no one cares to produce simply to enrich others without benefit to himself. Secure and equitable Constitutional Government, therefore, is one of the first conditions of material advancement. In this respect New South Wales offers all the advantages of the Mother Country, with all the additional benefit of freedom from the relics of the feudal system which still linger in the European States and impede the progress of the people. Until the year 1856 New South Wales was in the condition of a Crown Colony, but in that year the present Constitution Act came into force, and ever since the people have governed themselves, by representative institutions based on the model of the English Parliament. The Queen is the head of the State, and in her name all legal business is transacted. Every Act of the Local Parliament, to be valid, must receive her assent, through her Representative the Governor, and in certain cases affecting Imperial interests Bills are reserved for the Royal assent. It is rarely, however, that this power of veto reserved to the Sovereign is exercised, and the assent of the Governor in nearly all cases of legislation is sufficient. The Parliament consists of two Houses: the Legislative Assembly of seventy-two Members, elected by the people and holding their seats for five years, and a Legislative Council of thirty-one Members nominated for life by the Governor in Council. A Bill for the reform of the Upper House is now before the Parliament, the purport of which is to base the Council on popular representation. The Governor is assisted by an Executive Council of seven Members, always consisting of the Ministers who hold the higher offices of State for the time-being, and no Ministry can long exist without a Parliamentary majority.

The Legislative Assembly, like the British House of Commons, is the actual governing body, and this House is open to all citizens without religious or property distinction of any kind, and the poorest and lowest in social rank may win by ability and good character the highest offices of State. The terms of the Electoral Act defining the qualifications of Members are these: Every male subject of Her Majesty of the full age of twenty-one years, and absolutely free, being natural born, or who being a naturalized subject, shall have resided in this Colony for five years, shall be qualified to be elected a Member of the Assembly for any Electoral District unless disqualified by section 17 or 18 of the Constitution Act or unless under section 11 or 12 of this Act he would be disqualified or incapacitated as an elector. The following is the qualification of electors:—" Every male subject of Her Majesty of the full age of twenty-one years, being natural born, or who, being a naturalized subject, shall have resided in this Colony for three years, shall, if qualified as in this section is provided, and entered on the roll of electors, and not disqualified or incapacitated for some cause hereinafter specified, be entitled to vote at any election for the Electoral District in respect of which he shall be so qualified." The qualification required in the section is six months residence in the Electorate, or a freehold estate of the annual value of £10. The persons disqualified are criminals, paupers, the insane, soldiers, and police. There is an annual revision of the Electoral Roll made by Government, by means of the police. One of the greatest boons to the Country for securing quietness and fairness of election is vote by ballot. However excited the populace may be, and whatever question may be pending, election riots are quite unknown; and though a few instances of personation occur, they are extremely rare, and bribery is all but impossible. In no part of the World have the people greater political equality, and nowhere can they exercise their rights and privileges with greater freedom, independence, and security. To examine critically the whole of legislation since the passing of the Constitution Act is not the scope of these pages; but, as instances of the practical wisdom of government, we may cite the Public Schools Act, the Acts alienating the Public Lands, the Municipalities Act, and others adapted to the wants and calculated to advance the moral condition and various industries of the Country. The defects of government, if we may legitimately refer to them, arise necessarily from the smallness of the community and the vastness of the area for which measures have to be provided. Every increase of population will lessen the difficulty of government, and increase the power of the Colony for useful and progressive legislation. New South Wales offers to all intelligent, sensible, and industrious immigrants a fair field and no favour, politically and socially; and it is absolutely certain that many able men who are buried in obscurity in the old Countries, and can never rise out of their social encumbrances so as to make themselves heard, may become here men of mark and power, and leave their names written out in the annals of their Country as the leaders and benefactors of their race. All who cherish so worthy an ambition may confer a greater boon on their Country by casting in their lot with the Colonies, than by remaining in obscurity and indigence in their native land.

III.—AGRICULTURAL SETTLEMENT.

How to get Land.

THE great diversity of our climate, and the richness of the soil over large tracts of country, afford the most tempting inducements to agricultural settlement in New South Wales. The profitable character of other pursuits, however, and the almost exclusive occupation of the country for grazing purposes, have caused farming to be very much neglected; and it is only within a very recent period that the colonists have been able to form any adequate idea of the productive character and varied capabilities of the land in districts more remote from the Capital. In 1861 the Parliament passed an Act for regulating the Alienation of Crown Lands. That Act is still law, and it offers very great facilities for the acquirement of land by men of small means. Anybody is at liberty to take up any quantity of the best land he can discover, between 40 acres and 320 acres, at £1 an acre; and, on payment of one-fourth of the purchase money he obtains undisturbed possession. He is not dependent upon the caprice of any official; and he need not wait to have his land surveyed, although, as a matter of fact, the surveyor will speedily follow him, and definitely determine the boundaries of his estate. If the land conterminous to his own have not been alienated from the Crown, the conditional purchaser is entitled by law to depasture his stock over an area three times the size of his purchase. This "grazing right," as it is called, cannot, however, be relied on with any degree of certainty, for, in the progress of settlement, these grazing areas are speedily converted into freehold homesteads by successive conditional purchasers. As soon as the whole of the purchase money has been paid, the Government issues the title, which is indefeasible; for it must be remembered that Torrens' Act is in force in this Colony, and titles to land once registered under it can never be called in question. The interest (5 per cent.) payable on the unpaid balance of three-fourths of the purchase money, is equivalent to a yearly rental of one shilling for every acre conditionally purchased. The following are the words of the Act which provide for the conditional sale of unimproved lands without competition:—

On and from the first day of January one thousand eight hundred and sixty-two Crown Lands other than town lands or suburban lands and not being within a proclaimed Gold Field nor under lease for mining purposes to any person other than the applicant for purchase and not being within areas bounded by lines bearing north east south and west and distant ten miles from the outside boundary of any city or town containing according to the then last census ten thousand inhabitants or five miles to the outside boundary of any town containing according to the then last census five thousand inhabitants or three miles from the outside boundary of any town containing according to the then last census one thousand inhabitants or two miles from the outside boundary of any town or village containing according to the then last census one hundred inhabitants and not reserved for the site of any town or village or for the supply of water or from sale for any public purpose and not containing improvements and not excepted from sale under section seven of this Act shall be open for conditional sale by selection in the manner following (that is to say) Any person may upon any Land Office day tender to the Land Agent for the district a written application for the conditional purchase of any such lands not less than forty acres nor more than three hundred and twenty acres at the price of twenty shillings per acre and may pay to such Land Agent a deposit of twenty-five per centum of the purchase money thereof And if no other like application and deposit for the same land be tendered at the same time such person shall be declared the conditional purchaser thereof at the price aforesaid Provided that if more than one such application and deposit for the same land or any part thereof shall be tendered at the same time to such Land Agent he shall unless all such applications but one be immediately withdrawn forthwith proceed to determine by lot in such manner as may be prescribed by Regulations made under this Act which of the applicants shall become the purchaser.

It will be seen that the only restrictions upon choice are those which are absolutely necessary for the protection of the public interests. In consideration, however, of the liberal terms upon which land may thus be obtained, other sections of the Act require that the conditional purchaser shall reside upon his land for a period of three years, and during that time make improvements to the value of £1 an acre—conditions implying no practical hardship upon the *bonâ fide* settler, and which are fully satisfied by the exercise of his own labour. The Act came into operation on the 1st of January, 1862, and from that date to the 31st December, 1871, 2,849,391 acres were conditionally purchased by 37,216 applicants—and that is probably the best proof that could be adduced of the beneficial operation of the law. Much of the land thus alienated has been brought under the dominion of the plough.

Pioneer Work.

Twenty-five pounds thus enable a man to acquire a homestead of 100 acres. The cost of agricultural implements is a trifle greater in this Colony than in England; but it is necessary that the farmer should have money enough to provide himself with rations until such time as he can reap a harvest from his land; and, if he have cash enough to buy a horse and cart (or a boat, if his land be upon the banks of a river), and to provide himself with a cow, a few pigs, sheep, and poultry, he is practically independent of all the world, for he has resources within his own domain which will enable him to more than supply all his legitimate wants, and to convey his surplus produce to a market. Nothing is more common in this genial climate than to see carriers and drovers sleeping out, with the heavens as their only canopy. Upon all the roads, lodging-houses and hotels occur at convenient intervals; and yet, such is the force of habit and the fascination of the camp fire, that teamsters prefer this rough freedom, and find the shelter of their drays sufficient. What is of consequence is, that "camping out" does not seem to have any injurious effect upon the health of those who thus expose themselves to the night air; so that shelter from the rain, which can be provided in a few hours, is all that is absolutely needed in the way of lodging in the first instance. The man, however, whose ambition it is to make a home for his family and to acquire influence as a citizen, is not content with bare shelter; and his first care, therefore, is to build himself a snug house, and to enclose his ground. His land supplies him with timber for both purposes, and all the trouble he is put to is the labour of felling and shaping it. Bark for the roof is obtainable in any length, from several descriptions of forest trees which grow in every part of the Colony, and it makes a capital covering—impervious to the rain, warm, and durable. Should the settler have to resort to hired labour, a substantial and comfortable structure of four rooms will probably cost him about £20. His dwelling will have no pretensions to architectural embellishment, but will be quite as presentable as many of those which are thought good enough for the occupation of farm labourers in the Mother Country, and being suited to the climate, will be far more healthy. In only few parts of New South Wales, and those of very limited area, does winter visit us with the rigour which involves the poor of Britain and Northern Europe in so much privation and distress. In the Coast Districts, and in many other parts of the Colony, the farmer does not need to spend a farthing on the erection of sheds for the shelter of his stock; and the operations of the husbandman are never suspended by frost or snow. Over a large extent of country, crops are produced in succession from January to December; and some descriptions of produce—French beans, for example—may be had fresh from the garden nine months out of the twelve.

The Settler's Home.

The character of the settler's home depends entirely upon himself, for neither scarcity of materials nor cost of labour offer any insuperable obstacle to its being made as comfortable as heart could wish. Many are content to live in rude habitations, and disregard external appearances; but every year brings with it improvement. Passion-vines, loaded every six months with globes of luscious fruit, clothe the outbuildings of many a humble tenement with foliage, glossy and green through summer and winter. The grape-vine, with its massive clusters of yellow and purple fruit trailing over the verandahs, gives a grateful shade during summer and autumn to many a country home; while the settler who is less utilitarian in his ideas may, if he prefers it, inhale the fragrance of the honeysuckle or the rose, or embower his habitation in the glowing hues of the Bignonia, the Bougainvillea, or other gorgeous climbers which elsewhere unfold their floral magnificence only under the costly nurture of the conservatory. With the increase of family life comes an increase of refinement, and the multiplication of comforts. Flower gardens and orchards are the produce of a few hours leisure, and nothing is more pleasing in the spring of the year than to see the agricultural homesteads which are dotted over the face of the country enveloped in the pink and white blossoms of the peach, the plum, the apricot, the nectarine, the apple, and the pear, which rest like a cloud upon the landscape, flushing it with warmth and beauty. Such is the exuberance of all descriptions of fruit-trees in this country that a very small patch of ground gives abundance for summer use, and more than enough for the consumption of the year, if it be thought worth while to dry, bottle, or preserve it.

The Farmer's Prospects.

The state of farming in New South Wales cannot be compared with that of the Mother Country, where agriculture has become a science, and where the farmer has commonly the advantages of large capital and easy access to unlimited markets. There are few large farmers in the Colony, and the steam plough has not yet been seen in more than one district. There is, however, plenty of level land well adapted to steam cultivation, and there is no reason why farming on a large scale should not be highly remunerative, now that the three principal lines of Railway have almost reached the rich wheat-growing districts in the west, north, and south. A very large proportion of the cultivators of the soil in this Colony began life with little capital and less experience,—under conditions which in any other calling or Country would have rendered failure inevitable ; and that they have not failed is the best proof of the favourable conditions under which agriculture may be carried on. Instances might be mentioned of men who have acquired fortunes. A gentleman, who was for many years a Minister of the Crown, stated before a Parliamentary Committee : " I know instances of men in the Hunter District who have made thousands and tens of thousands by agriculture. I believe the people of the Western Districts obtained their wealth in the first instance by agriculture. Their stock increased in numbers and value until the owners became enormously wealthy, independent of their agriculture, and then they gave up the cultivation of the land, as far as they were personally concerned." The Clarence is one of the latest districts taken up for farming purposes, and the settlers there have generally been very successful. Mr. B. began with a capital of £100 upon a freehold farm of 50 acres in 1857. He is now the owner of several valuable farms, a number of superior well-bred cattle, and has £3,000 and upwards invested in various securities. Another farmer, A. D., bought land from the Government in the same year. In two years his farm repaid him the amount of the purchase money, and the cost of labour in clearing and cultivating. He is now the owner of some of the best land in the district, and is thoroughly independent. Two single men, having a joint capital of £40, took up a farm of dense brush land, 70 acres in extent, on a clearing lease for five years. At the end of the period they had each earned upwards of £400. In New South Wales, however, as probably in every other part of the World, agriculture is a slower, but at the same time, a surer road to competence than most other pursuits. In England, the agricultural labourer is too often poorly paid and badly fed. He spends his years in one perpetual conflict with poverty, if not with starvation ; and when at last he can no longer keep the wolf from the door, his heritage is a dispensation of parish pay. In

New South Wales, two or three years of industry and frugality will put the farm labourer in possession of money enough to ensure a fair start in life as a proprietor and cultivator of the soil; and a few more years of intelligent, well-directed toil will enable him to establish a home for himself and his family, and that, too, while he is in the constant enjoyment of all the comforts of life, and while his children are receiving an education in the Public Schools of the Country which may qualify them to occupy the highest positions of influence and power in the community. It cannot for a moment be pretended that the farmer in New South Wales is exempt from the common lot of labour. If any man will not work, neither should he eat. The vicissitudes of climate, and the prevalence of insect life which preys upon his crops, have to be encountered here as elsewhere, but they are not more formidable. Patience, industry, and skill conquer all obstacles, and the man is physically, intellectually, and morally the better for the conflict. As he sows, so he reaps. He is never out of employment; his anxieties are "the ordinary vicissitudes of more or less; his cares are, that he takes his fair share of the business of life,—that he is a free human being, and not perpetually a child. He is no longer a being of a different order from the middle classes. He has pursuits like those which occupy them, and give to their intellects the greatest part of such cultivation as they receive."

A reference to the Agricultural Map, which is bound up with this pamphlet, will enable the reader to see at a glance the localities in which the leading crops of the Colony have been successfully cultivated. Hitherto the farmers have commonly confined their attention to one particular crop, but it is not likely that they will long be dependent upon any one cereal production. As experience is gained, a better system of cultivation obtains, and in some parts of the Colony the value of a rotation of crops, and the necessity for manuring soils long cultivated, are beginning to be understood and acted upon. Many of those who began with small holdings of forty acres have now obtained the maximum limit obtainable under conditional purchase (320 acres), and have added grazing to the ordinary occupations of the farm.

Wheat.

In the early days of the Colony wheat was grown extensively in the valleys of the Hunter and the Hawkesbury, in the vicinity of Campbelltown and Camden; but in those localities wheat has now been very largely superseded by other crops. It is on the table lands that the best wheat-growing districts occur. The country lying to the north of Murrurundi is admirably adapted for its growth, and in the neighbourhood of Tamworth, Armidale, and Inverell, there is a large acreage under this crop. In the Western District, Orange may be taken as the centre of a very large extent of wheat-growing country; and similarly, Young in the south-west, and Tumut, which lies still further to the southward. These districts are from 2,000 to 4,000 feet above sea-level, and they contain an extent of rich agricultural land which is capable of producing all the wheat needed for the support of a population of many millions. Rust, which often proves fatal to the wheat crops on the coast, is unknown in the Southern District, of which Tumut may be taken as a centre, or in the West, with Orange as its principal market. Crops of fifty-two bushels to the acre have been obtained near Inverell; but while the soil in that neighbourhood is exceptionally rich, the climate is more variable. The average yield of last year's crop, according to the Returns furnished by the police, was from 14 to 15 bushels to the acre; but from the cultivation of the wheat lands in the south and the west an average of 25 bushels may be counted on, even with the comparatively unskilled farming which is still prevalent. The local newspaper states that the wheat crop in the Monaro District this season (1872-3) has been garnered, and has averaged from 40 to 60 bushels per acre on some of the richest lands. We should say here, once for all, that the agricultural statistics of the Country are collected by the Police; but it is a fact known to the head of that Department that the produce of the crops are almost invariably understated by the settlers. Nothing is more common than for a farmer to tell the constable who asks him for information about his crop, that his wheat, for instance, has averaged 10 bushels per acre, when, in point of fact, he has taken 20 or 25 bushels per acre to the mill-owner. The value of accurate statistics, and the purpose for which they are asked, are often not understood by persons of this class, and they are apt to regard the questions put them as an impertinent inquisition into their private affairs. Then, too, the cultivation is often slovenly in the extreme; and, as the stumps of the forest trees are left standing above the ground, a large portion of every acre never comes under cultivation at all, and more particularly is this the case where the roots of the trees branch out on the surface of the soil. Deep ploughing and rotation of crops are as yet by no means general. It is estimated that a very large proportion of this year's crop will yield from 30 to 35 bushels an acre. One of the oldest residents in the Western Districts (Mr. W. H. Suttor), speaking before a Committee of the Legislative Assembly, two years ago, of the wheat crop in the Orange District, said: "I never knew a failure of the wheat crop there." Similar testimony might be adduced respecting other districts. The following statement is clipped from the *Bathurst Free Press* of January, 1873, and refers to the harvest of the present year :—

Several reports have reached us to the effect that if they had been able to save the crop, some of the farmers would have been able to house from 30 to 50 bushels to the acre. Mr. James Cock, miller, of this city, informs us that he has purchased from Mr. Plummer, of Alloway Bank, 568 bushels of new wheat, the produce of his ground, being at the rate of 29 bushels to the acre. Mr. James Seage, of O'Connell Plains, about Christmas time, stripped some of his crop, which yielded 25 bushels to the acre ; but the ground has been rendered so soft by the late rains that stripping machines could not be taken on to the ground, or a larger amount of grain would no doubt have been gathered into the barn during the fine weather.

For many years the consumption of wheat and flour in the interior was chiefly supplied by grain imported from South Australia and America; but all the inland markets are now supplied by local production, and there is a considerable export of New South Wales flour across the Border into Southern Queensland, and from the Albury District into Victoria. In the course of a year or two it is expected that the whole of our markets will be supplied with wheat grown in the Colony, and that we shall have a considerable surplus for export. At present our foreign supplies are chiefly drawn from South Australia, where, however, the average crop for the last ten years has been less than ten bushels to the acre. Last year's imports from the sister Colony were to the value of £260,346. The value of the imports of wheat and flour, deducting exports, has averaged £472,560; and if grain of all kinds used for food be added, the excess of imports over exports has been at the rate of £538,000 for each of the last ten years. No scientific analysis of the wheat grown in different parts of the Colony has been made ; but there is no reason to suppose that the wheat grown in New South Wales is at all inferior to that produced elsewhere.

A sample of wheat grown near Bathurst gained the prize medal in the Great Exhibition of 1862. It weighed 69½ lbs. per bushel; the average weight of wheat grown in the district being 64 or 65 lbs. The average price of wheat in Sydney was 5s. 1d. for 1871.

Maize and Maizena.

One of the most extensive and prolific crops grown in the Colony is that of Maize, or Indian Corn. In America this commodity enters largely into consumption as an article of human food; but in this Colony it is principally used as horse food. The manufactured article, maizena, or corn flour, has established itself in the colonial markets, and there is a considerable demand for it, at a retail price of 6d. or 7d. a pound. Maize is cultivated as far south as Moruya, in latitude 36° S., and it is grown all through the Coast Districts to the northern boundary of the Colony. Last year, the average reported yield of the whole crop of the Colony was 34 bushels to the acre. On the rich scrub lands of the Clarence River the first crops (after the timber has been burnt off) average from 100 to 120 bushels to the acre; and with reasonably good farming the average of subsequent crops has been 65 bushels to the acre in that district. There is a steady demand for maize in the neighbouring Colonies. Last year Victoria took 87,519 bushels, and New Zealand 14,386 bushels; our total export of maize being 732,657 bushels and bags, the estimated value of which was £109,412. Nothing can be more simple than the cultivation of maize, and it is a crop which matures quickly. Thus, in the County of Camden, for example, maize sown in October is ready for harvesting from February to April; and some varieties sown in November are ready for harvesting early in February. It appears to be free from the attacks of insects and fungi. A failure of the crop is never known, and on the alluvial banks of some of our rivers it has been grown year after year for a quarter of a century and upwards. The average price of maize in the Sydney market is 2s. 6d. a bushel.

Sugar: Growth and Manufacture.

For many years it has been known to a few persons that the Sugar-cane would grow well over a large area of the Colony; but its cultivation was a thing so foreign to the experience of farmers, that it was not until five years ago that attention was fairly

c

directed to the profitable character of this industry. In 1867 the land under sugar cultivation was 116 acres, and the produce of it was 17,780 lbs. In 1871 the breadth of land under sugar was 4,394 acres, and the portion of the crop ready for crushing (1,995 acres) gave a return of 2,780,288 lbs.; but this quantity is exclusive of 748 acres of cane grown in the Clarence District, the produce of which was not ascertained. Taking the population of the Colony at 527,682 souls, and the average consumption of sugar at 60 lbs. per head (which is a low average), the quantity of sugar required for our own consumption at the present time is 31,660,920 lbs.; so that, rapid as have been the strides which this industry has made in New South Wales, there is still ample scope for expansion, and we require a considerable augmentation of farm labour for this industry alone before we shall be in a position to compete in the markets of the World. The cultivation of the sugar-cane is easy; and the experience of the last few years justifies the most sanguine expectations for the future. The cost of cultivation for the first crop, which will be ready for cutting in twenty-three months, is about £11 an acre, and of subsequent crops, which take thirteen months to mature, about £5. On good level land the yield should be from 40 to 55 tons per acre. The large manufactories have only been at work three seasons, so that experience does not go beyond three crops, but in some few places on the Clarence there are small patches of cane which have been cut five or six times, and show no signs of giving out. The average yield per acre for two-year-old cane crushed at the large mills on the Clarence has been about 32 tons; but in parts of the district the cultivation has been so miserable until lately that this average does not give a fair idea of what can be done by the most ordinary farming. It is estimated that by merely keeping the weeds down and the cane well trashed, an average of forty tons could easily be reached for two-year-old cane, and 24 and 22 tons for first and second ratoons (or third and fourth crops) respectively. By draining the soil and applying lime, much higher results would be obtained. The heaviest crops cut have averaged 58½ tons of cane to the acre. The manufacturers pay the grower 15s. a ton for his cane delivered at the mills, or 10s. per ton if the mill owners cut and cart it away themselves. A gentleman having some experience as a manufacturer and grower writes: "The average yield will be about 35 tons per acre, although there are some favourable spots along the banks of the Clarence which will yield from 60 to 70 tons per acre. An acre of two-year-old cane well cared for from planting to maturity will yield about 2½ tons of sugar, at 35 tons of cane per acre; but if the best appliances for manufacture be used, higher results would be obtained." Other growers state the yield to be at 60 tons for first crop, and 40 tons for the second; but results no doubt mainly depend upon quality of soil and character of cultivation. Mr. Angus Mackay, in his work entitled "The Sugar-cane in Australia," writes: "The cost of making sugar varies much according to the condition of the canes and the system on which the business is conducted. Grey rations, on a large scale (worth fully £34 per ton) have been made during this last season at about £3 per ton. That is the total cost from the time the canes were cut in the field. The whole cost of growing and making was about £12 10s. per ton." Good yellow counter sugar is sold wholesale in the Sydney market at from £30 to £36 a ton.

The Sugar-cane thrives in many parts of the Colony, but its cultivation and the manufacture of sugar are at present principally carried on between the 32nd parallel of latitude and the northern boundary of the Colony. The banks of the Manning, the Macleay, the Clarence, the Richmond, and the Tweed, are the chief seats of the sugar industry; but the growth of the cane has also been commenced in the Murrumbidgee District, and is destined to assume vast proportions. The Colonial Sugar Company have built three large mills, at the cost of many thousand pounds for each; there are also a large number of small mills, owned by growers who prefer to crush their own cane. In 1871, there were 52 mills in the Colony, which manufactured 35,836 cwt. of sugar, and 113,151 cwt. of molasses. In the last four years the value of the sugar produced from cane grown in the Colony exceeded £150,000.

But the Colony need not be dependent on the cane alone, for experiments have shown that Sorghum or Imphee is capable of producing a large yield of sugar. This plant is easily cultivated, and thrives well in many parts of the Colony, where the Sugar-cane would be cut off by frost. The manufacture was commenced about a year ago on a small scale in the Hunter River District; but as the manufacturer had not the means to purchase crops from the farmers they ceased to grow them. Mr. Leonard Wray describes the advantages of sorghum for the production of sugar in the following terms :—" 1. It takes from three to four and a half months, according to the kind planted, from the time of sowing the seed until it arrives at maturity; and it will ratoon twice or three times afterwards, at intervals of three months between each cutting, provided of course that the warm weather permits their continued ratooning. 2. It is much more juicy than the generality of sugar-canes, and contains far less woody fibre, which does not materially increase in the ratoons. 3. Fine average imphœ juice contains 15 per cent. of sugar. 4. A good average crop of imphee stalks or canes will weigh 25 tons per acre. 5. Imphee is produced from the seed, therefore no deterioration can occur. 6. It will yield a crop of ratoons six to seven months from the time of the seed being first sown, being therefore two crops in that space of time, and will continue ratooning if the seasons are favourable." In New South Wales imphœ is almost exclusively grown as food for cattle, for which purpose it is highly esteemed.

Beet-root also grows well in many districts of the Colony, more particularly in the South-eastern coast, but at present is only grown for feeding stock.

The Vine: Wine-making.

New South Wales contains millions of acres of soil admirably adapted for the growth of the grape, of which nearly every European variety is rooted in the Colony, and the produce of her vineyards may vie with those of the most favoured countries of Southern Europe. If there is one fruit which luxuriates in this sunny clime more than another, it is the grape. The wines of the Albury District, on the Murray, are famous throughout Australia, and the produce of the Hunter River and New England country has been awarded many medals at the great International Exhibitions of London and Paris. All through the Coast Districts the grape flourishes, and generously rewards the grower. It is to be found in nearly every garden, and as an article of diet it is within the reach of the poorest in the land.

The consumption of Colonial wine increases year by year, and it is thought that the wines of New South Wales would compete successfully with the light wines of France in the English market, were they admitted at the same rate of duty. Last year our vignerons manufactured 413,321 gallons of wine, and 1,766 gallons of brandy. The quantity of grapes produced for table use from vineyards exceeding one acre in extent was 508 tons.

Wine-growing is a very profitable branch of agriculture in the Colony, and may reasonably be expected, with the growth of population, to be more so. It does not confine its rewards to the large capitalist, but will amply remunerate the man of small means who has the requisite skill and industry to enter upon it. One man can attend to eight or ten acres of vineyard, by obtaining occasional assistance; and if he have any mechanical ability, he can, as many of the small growers, who are chiefly Germans, now do, make most of his plant himself. Should he have to buy the plant, he will need a capital of from £50 to £100. A handy man who could do his own coopering would require less. A small grower could not reckon on more than from 300 to 500 gallons of wine per acre. The largest manufacturer in the Hunter District has, in favourable seasons, and from certain kinds of grapes, obtained a thousand gallons per acre, but his average yield would not be more than from 600 to 700 gallons. Much depends upon the soil and the variety of grape. Five hundred gallons must be considered a good average yield. A well-known author, writing on the culture of the vine in New South Wales, says: "At 400 gallons to the acre, and 2s. per gallon for his wine-juice, the vigneron would get £40 per acre, and 100 acres of vineyard would yield £4,000 a year, leaving ample margin for causalties. The labour in a vineyard may be reduced to a small percentage on the produce, by planting in such a manner that it can be ploughed in various directions, and by using suitable implements."

Tobacco: Growth and Manufacture.

Tobacco is grown chiefly on the Paterson, the Williams, and their tributaries, in the Hunter River District, and there are also small areas under cultivation in the Clarence and the Murrumbidgee. The crop is more precarious than any other in the Hunter Valley, where it has been chiefly tried, and the price also fluctuates considerably. Frost and wet are sometimes fatal to it. One man can cultivate three acres, from which the average return would be twelve cwt., and the price which he would get for his leaf would be 5d. and 6d. per lb. Formerly, Colonial tobacco was exclusively used as a sheep-wash; but, with improved cultivation and manufacture, it is finding its way into the favour of smokers, and a steady demand for it has now grown up. It is still, however, much inferior to the Virginian leaf, which is imported in large quantities and made up in the Colony. There are about three hundred men and boys employed in the Sydney factories alone; and one of the largest manufacturers of tobacco in the World, the proprietor of the Raven brand, is now fitting up a very large factory in Sydney; and we have the prospect of a considerable export trade in this commodity. The tobacco grown in the Colony in 1871 amounted to 4,476 cwt., and the quantity manufactured was 6,367 cwt.

Cereal and other Crops.

Barley, oats, rye, and other cereal crops, grow as well in New South Wales, on the table-lands, as in England, and the acreage has considerably increased of late years. They are, however, largely grown for fodder, and the requirements of the Colony for grain of this description are not nearly met. According to the official returns for 1872 the barley crop covered 3,461 acres, the produce of which were 55,284 bushels. The breadth of land under oats was 13,795 acres, and the produce 280,887 bushels; rye, 1,342 acres, and the produce 17,339 bushels; millet, 254 acres, and the produce 4,346 bushels. We draw large supplies of potatoes from the southern Colonies. Our own cultivation is chiefly on the south-east coast. The 14,770 acres under this crop last year gave 44,758 tons, or an average of over 3 tons to the acre. There are many parts of the interior where the potato produces heavy crops, but up to the present time the cost of carriage has prevented inland growers from taking advantage of the Sydney market. Potato disease is unknown in New South Wales.

A great deal of hay (oats, wheat, barley, and lucerne) is grown in the colony. Last year's crop covered 51,805 acres, and gave 77,459 tons. Lucerne hay is mostly grown on the Hawkesbury and the Hunter; and so admirably adapted is this plant to our soil and climate, that on the alluvial banks of the Hunter it may be cut six times in the year in ordinary seasons. Pumpkins are another prolific crop, and, in the more thickly settled districts, are coming into use as food for cattle. Mangold-wurzel, and, to a very limited extent, turnips, are grown for the same purpose. It is very rarely the case that farmers take the trouble to feed any but the choicest cattle, the ordinary herds of the Colony being left to fatten on the natural grasses.

SEMI-TROPICAL PRODUCTIONS.

Some attention is being paid to the growth of arrowroot, and last year's crop of twenty-six acres produced 26,454 lbs. The soil of our northern rivers is especially well adapted for its growth, and indeed for the growth of many other semi-tropical productions. On this point the opinion of one of our foremost colonists (the Rev. J. D. Lang, D.D.), may be read with advantage, for it is the deduction of one who has travelled far and seen much. He says:—"It would be difficult indeed to find a more eligible country for the settlement of a numerous agricultural population than the banks of the Clarence, the Richmond, and the Tweed, in New South Wales. Whether for the small farmer, who would purchase and cultivate with his own hands a farm of from twenty to eighty acres, or for families of superior standing in society who could afford to purchase for their own settlement in the country one or two square miles (640 or 1,280 acres) of land, and to employ hired labourers—all of which could be done with a very moderate amount of capital—or for capitalists intending to embark largely in the cultivation of cotton, or other tropical productions suited to the soil and climate, I am persuaded there is no place in the World which at this moment presents a more eligible field or a more favourable prospect."

DRIED FRUITS.

There are other departments of agricultural industry for which the soil and climate of New South Wales are eminently fitted, but to which little attention has as yet been paid. Sir William Macarthur has demonstrated the fact that the olive and the caper grow well at Camden, and from the former has manufactured very pure samples of oil. He has also prepared raisins, currants, prunes, and many descriptions of dried fruits, from his estate, and these commodities have been quite equal to the best imported articles. His efforts, however, in these directions have been the recreations of a country gentleman far advanced in years; and nothing has yet been done to make fruits grown and dried in the Colony a marketable commodity. New South Wales still offers a fine field for the industries of Southern Europe; and those who have the requisite skill to turn the bountiful gifts of Providence to practical account may well inquire whether they can obtain so large a reward for their labour as that which this Colony ensures.

Vegetable Fibres, &c.

Nothing whatever has yet been done to develop the resources of the Colony in regard to vegetable products suitable for the manufacture of dyes, fibres, and paper. The New Zealand flax (*Phormium tenax*) is grown in all the gardens of the Colony, and so also is the grass-cloth plant (*Bœhmeria nivea*), and these, to say nothing of many other fibre plants, ought to become important sources of wealth to this Country. The growth of the Acacia for tanning purposes has been often recommended as a profitable industry. This handsome tree, in almost all its varieties, is indigenous to New South Wales, but whole forests have been well nigh exterminated for their bark, and the tanneries of the Colony, which are the basis of a very large industry here, are now largely dependent upon imported bark. Our population, however, is so small compared with the magnitude of our resources, that these branches of agriculture will probably have to remain for some time longer in the category of postponed industries.

Sericulture.

The Colony possesses special advantages for sericulture. The Italian, French, Egyptian, and other varieties of silkworm, have been produced without any trace of diseases which prove so destructive in Southern Europe; and we have all the descriptions of vegetable food they can require. Mr. Charles Brady, in a letter addressed to the Colonial Secretary, dated Sydney, 17th March, 1870, says:—"My own personal knowledge and experience in the treatment of silkworms in New South Wales and Queensland for several years, justify me in expressing my conviction that this part of Australia, at any rate, is peculiarly well adapted for the production of cocoons. I began the study of the subject in 1862, and have since devoted myself exclusively to this pursuit, in all its relations, particularly to experiments and efforts to take advantage of our brilliant atmosphere, and of various food grown in this climate, to introduce and breed superior races of silkworms, and especially to free them from the dire disease which now for so many years has all but destroyed an industry yielding annually more than thirty millions of pounds sterling to the present cultivators of Southern Europe. My experiences have been most conclusive and satisfactory, and it is proved that the importance of our proceedings here is not unappreciated in England by persons capable of forming an estimate of their value. I am well aware that the public mind is prepossessed with the idea that the growth of silk in Australia must prove unremunerative on account of the high relative price of labour in the Colonies; but I have never met with even one person who had investigated the subject, or qualified himself in any way to form an opinion, who held this idea; in fact, there not only is nothing to prevent silk being raised as cheaply in Australia as in France or Italy, but there is very good reason to believe that, favoured as we are by climate and cheap land, we may be in a position to undersell any Country in Europe."

Mr. Brady has orders for all the grain he can produce · and he has just started in the industry on the Tweed River where, it is hoped, his glowing anticipations may be fully realized.

Fruits, &c.

The lines of ocean steamships which run daily along our northern and southern coasts, and the Railways which connect the metropolis with the cool table-lands to the west, pour into the markets of Sydney all the fruits of temperate and semi-tropical climes. In the immediate neighbourhood of the capital there are orange groves as magnificent as any which have ever gladdened the eyes of tourists in Spain or Portugal; and there are few pictures of greater beauty than the vine-clad hills and extensive orange plantations around Parramatta, fourteen miles by railway from Sydney, or than the miniature forests of orange trees which crown the ridges all along the winding course of the river, and which, in some places, slope down to the margin of the stream. The Parramatta River is in fact an arm of the sea, and is one of the many inlets of Port Jackson, forming pictures of enchanting loveliness, and which only lack the historical associations and rugged peaks of the Rhine to make them far more famous. A fleet of steamers ply hourly between Sydney and

Parramatta, calling at numerous picturesque villages, the residence of merchants and professional men, and where the soil is devoted almost exclusively to the growth of the orange, strawberries, and stone fruits, for the Sydney market. The orange and other members of the citron family also flourish luxuriantly in the valleys of the Hunter and the Clarence, and indeed all through the coast districts, over a belt of country about three hundred miles from north to south. Many proprietors of orangeries have reaped a fortune; and although the price of the fruit is very low, its growth is still remunerative. Every year we export between £40,000 and £50,000 worth of oranges alone to Victoria and the other Colonies, where the cultivation of this fruit does not appear to be attended with much success. Some of the trees at Parramatta, forty years old, have attained a height of 35 feet, and their branches a circumference of nearly 100 feet; and in the year 1859 as many as 12,000 oranges were obtained from individual trees. The produce, of course, varies with the age, size, and variety of the tree: but the crops are prolific, almost incredibly so to any one who has not seen this handsome tree in perfection. The Mandarin has borne 4,200 fruits in the year, and from the St. Michael (a larger variety) 1,200 oranges have been gathered in the twelve months.

Apples, pears, peaches, nectarines, plums, almonds, grapes, passion-vines, bananas, Chinese date plums (*Diospyros kaki*), cherries, quinces, loquats, strawberries, and all kinds of edible nuts—the ground nut (*Arachis hypogea*) among the number—grow well here. In the more temperate latitudes of the south we have gooseberries, raspberries, blackberries, currants, and every other description of what are here popularly called "English" fruits· while on the rivers in the northern part of the Colony, the banana, pineapple, custard apple (*Cherimoyer*) &c.. thrive best. The pineapple requires some slight protection from frosts, but the banana bears its fruit most abundantly all the year round. The other kinds of fruit named all yield exuberantly in New South Wales. We might add to the list of semi-tropical productions; for a large orchard devoted exclusively to this class of fruits has been planted on the Tweed River.

As to garden produce little need be said, for such has been the enthusiasm of some of our colonists in the direction of acclimatization that they have enriched the Country with all the valuable products of the Globe (excepting only the tropics) and there is no vegetable or fruit which conduces to the sustenance or pleasure of the human race which has not been introduced into New South Wales.

Occupation of the Soil.

According to the last Census, there were 43,805 persons engaged in agricultural pursuits, 17,835 in pastoral; 2,984 in horticultural; 246 in wine-growing; and 59 in sugar-growing. The total extent of freehold and leased land under occupation for agriculture was 7,855,067 acres, of which 417,851 were under cultivation, 3,921,505 acres were enclosed but not cultivated, and the remainder (3,515,711 acres) were not enclosed.

Waste Lands.

In the foregoing remarks we have enumerated most of the principal products of the soil which it has been proved can be cultivated with profit, but the catalogue must not be regarded as by any means complete. There are good grounds for believing that the Chincona-tree might be made the foundation of a considerable export trade to the Colony, and the same may be said of the Tea-tree, which has flourished in our midst for more than a generation. As yet, however, they have not been in any way practically tested. And, on the other hand, it must not be supposed that the whole Colony of New South Wales is a garden. The gifts of Nature have indeed been lavishly bestowed upon this fair Austral land; but there are large areas of country which are not suited for agriculture, and upon some regions the ban of sterility will probably rest for many years. Nevertheless, it is worthy of notice that of that long stretch of country falling from the table-land westward, little is known save that it is pastured by millions of sheep, and that the salt bush which covers it makes it the best fattening country we have. Of territory such as this, now worthless for agricultural settlement, the eminent botanist, Dr. F. Von Müeller, C.M.G., says:—" Let us translocate ourselves now for a moment to our desert tracts, changed, as they will likely be, many years hence, when the waters of the Murray River, in their unceasing flow from snowy sources, will be thrown over the back plains, and no longer run entirely into the ocean unutilized for husbandry. The lagoons may then be lined and the fertile depressions studded with the date palm; fig-trees, like in Egypt, planted by the hundreds of thousands, to increase and to retain the rain will then also have ameliorated here the climate; or the white mulberry-tree will be extensively extant then instead of the malle scrub; not to speak of the vine in endless variety, nor to allude to the copious culture of cotton in those regions."

AGRICULTURAL PRODUCE: SUPPLY AND DEMAND.

The following table shows that the agricultural production of the Colony has not yet overtaken the requirements of the inhabitants. It would be of interest if it simply indicated the extent to which the skill and labour of the husbandman may find profitable employment in supplying the demand for home consumption; but it is proper to point out that, as cheap and rapid Railway transit is being established with the richest agricultural lands of the interior, the growers of grain, wine, and other food-commodities, have opened to them the markets of the World in which to dispose of their surplus production.

BALANCE OF IMPORTS OVER EXPORTS—1871.

Arrowroot, Starch, &c.	£9,565	Oatmeal, Groats, &c.	£8,501
Bran	3,236	Onions	2,246
Confections & Preserves*	35,066	Pease	1,158
Flax and Hemp	10,521	Pickles, Sauces, &c.	18,935
Flour and Bread	194,019	Potatoes	37,642
Fruit (dried and bottled)	44,571	Hams, Bacon, &c.	3,500
Ditto (green)*	24,731	Sugar	407,406
Wheat	278,540	Tea	211,645
Oats	3,145	Tobacco and Cigars	47,857
Barley	655	Vinegar	5,207
Hay	2,002	Vegetables (green)	3,800
Hops	10,862	Wine	39,680
Malt	17,542		

* Chiefly from Tasmania.

IV.—PASTORAL OCCUPATION.

CHARACTER AND EXTENT.

WITHIN the duration of an ordinary life the flocks and herds of the early settlers of New South Wales have overspread nearly the whole of the vast Continent of Australia, until now they give a yearly income to this Colony alone of nearly £9,000,000, and represent a capital of about £30,000,000. In 1871 our live stock was equal to four head of cattle and thirty-two head of sheep for every man, woman, and child, in the community. At the present time (January, 1873), the returns of the Chief Inspector of Stock show that our sheep number about 18,000,000. But, multitudinous as our flocks and herds have become, nothing like justice has yet been done to the grazing capabilities of the Colony; for, out of about £3,000,000 spent on pastoral improvements, less than half a million sterling has been spent in the storage of water and the laying down of pasturage. When our vast territory shall have been redeemed from the state of nature in which it now lies, what limits shall be put to the production of wool and preserved meat! Markets for our wool have been established on the Continent of Europe, and in the Eastern and Western States of the American Union, as well as in the Mother Country; and the orders which have been sent for preserved meats have already outstripped our present ability to supply. There is still, therefore, ample room and verge enough in New South Wales for the profitable employment of capital and labour in this solid and prosperous industry.

The total area leased for pastoral purposes in 1871 was 138,409,520 acres, the great bulk of which is held on one and five years' leases respectively, and is open to the conditional purchaser to select from, under the terms stated in the last chapter. The pastoral holdings, or "squatting runs," as they are called in the Colony, range from 16,000 to 1,000,000 acres, and graze from 4,000 to 180,000 sheep. Many of the squatters have obtained enormous wealth as the reward of their enterprise in the pioneer settlement of the country. There are to-day a score of men who began life in this Colony as shepherds who are now worth from £30,000 to £50,000, and the wealth of some derived exclusively from pastoral pursuits exceeds a million pounds sterling. The yearly increase of the live stock owned by one gentleman in New South Wales is 12,000 calves and 50,000 lambs. The rent paid to the Government for the use of the land is from £30 to £800 per annum; the average of the total rent for 1871 being less than a halfpenny per acre over the whole Colony. The only condition which the Government requires from a person who takes up new country is practically this—that he shall put stock upon it, and turn it to beneficial use.

Sheep.

The fine-woolled sheep of the Colony came originally from the choicest flocks of France, Spain, and Saxony. The process of acclimatization has modified the original type of the Spanish merino. There has been a very decided gain in the softness of the wool, and an improvement in its elasticity. The wool has increased in length, but diminished in density, so that the weight of the fleece remains about the same. The average of last year's clip gave 4 lbs. 12 ozs. of greasy wool, or 2 lbs. 14 ozs. of washed wool, to the fleece. So admirably adapted is the climate of New South Wales for the production of fine wool, that experience has shown we have nothing to gain by the importation of stud sheep from Europe. The coarse-woolled sheep are chiefly depastured in the Coast District, where they thrive better than the merino. A flock of full-grown pure bred Leicesters will shear from 5 lbs. to 7 lbs. of washed wool per head, and lambs from three to four months old will cut from 3 lbs. to 4 lbs. of washed wool. Three-year-old wethers will weigh when killed from 160 to 200 lbs. each. It is in the country to the west of the main Dividing Range that the fine-woolled sheep are mostly depastured. Great success has attended the efforts made within the last few years to improve our flocks, so that the clip is not only better got up, but there is, on many stations, a younger, stronger, better-woolled, and a doubly valuable class of sheep, to that which existed five or six years ago. In some districts more than ninety per cent. of the lambs are saved. The average for the whole Colony in 1870 was 78½ per cent., and that result was obtained under a system as rough and negligent as could well exist.

Horned Cattle.

The breeding and fattening of cattle is also largely carried on, and in 1871 there were 2,014,888 head of horned cattle in the Colony. Short-horns and Herefords predominate. We have only one herd of Devons. Great attention has been paid to breeding, and our pedigree stock now numbers more than five thousand. The middling to first-class stock may be put down at 1,455,000, and the balance is inferior. Agricultural Societies now hold yearly exhibitions of stock and produce in every part of the Colony; and visitors from Europe tell us that the cattle at our leading shows would compare favourably with those shown at the

Provincial Exhibitions of the Royal Agricultural Society in England. The Intercolonial Exhibition held in Sydney in 1870 was attended by more than 184,000 persons. It is by no means uncommon to see pens of oxen, fattened on the natural grasses, weighing 1,500 lbs. each and occasionally animals appear whose weight exceeds 2000 lbs. Ordinarily well bred bullocks, however, will leave a good run at from 3½ to 4 years old, weighing from 700 lbs. to 800 lbs., and cows, 150 lbs. less. Their meat is generally excellent when killed, on or at a short distance from the station on which they are fed. It is comparatively fine in the grain, well flavoured, and fairly marbled. Foot and mouth disease, rinderpest, and other malignant diseases of cattle, are unknown in New South Wales.

Horses, Pigs, and Goats.

In 1871 our horse stock numbered 304,100, and pigs 213,193. All the best breeds exist in the Colony; but, in regard to horses, we have not yet recovered the deterioration which resulted from cross breeding and the dispersion of the best studs in the year of the gold discovery. An extensive trade for cavalry remount was at one time carried on with India; but it has now fallen into the hands of speculators, and is of a very uncertain character. There is still, however, a large demand for a really good description of horses, which this Colony is in an especial manner capable of supplying.

The llama and alpaca have been naturalized in the Colony; and in the Hunter District we have a flock of 1,200 Angora goats, a fleece from which, forwarded to England, sold for 2s. 6d. a pound. The clip from each goat weighs between 4 lbs. and 6 lbs. There are several smaller flocks in the hands of farmers in other parts of the Colony, and some attention is now being directed to their increase and management.

Preserved Meats.

In 1862 New South Wales exported 20 packages of preserved meats; in 1871 she exported 57,830 packages, of the total value of £152,950. £35,369 worth of this, however, was the produce of other Countries, so that the actual dimensions of our own manufacture are 47,870 packages, and the value £133,266. The first meat-preserving establishment in Australia commenced operations on the Clarence River in 1866, and its manufactures entered largely into consumption during the Franco-German war. It employs 150 men, and "works up" 1,000 head of cattle per month. Another large establishment belongs to the Sydney Company. It has been erected at a cost of £12,500, and is capable of producing 18,000 lbs. of preserved meat a day. There are nineteen salting and meat-preserving establishments in the Colony, and at nearly all the large factories Appert's and Liebig's processes are used. The following is a copy of the Sydney Company's printed list of prices for tinned meats, and the tins, of course, contain no bones :—Boiled beef, per lb., 5d.; ditto, corned, 5½d.; roasted beef, fresh, 5½d.; spiced ditto, 5½d.; tripe, plain, 6d.; ditto, with onions, 6d.; ox palates, 2 lb. tins, 7½d.; ox tongues, 4lb. tins, 2s. 6d.; boiled mutton, 5d.; roasted mutton, 6d.; haricot mutton, 6d.; sheep's tongues, 7½d.; Liebig's extract of meat, lb. tins, 7s. 6d.

Pastoral Progress.

Although great wealth has been amassed by the pastoral tenants of the Crown, yet, owing to the unimproved state of the country, the squatters are exposed to special risks; and in periods of drought they are sometimes overtaken by disastrous losses. If, however, a balance were struck, the profit would exceed the loss. The stability and expansiveness of this industry is proved by its steady and uniformly progressive development; and this is a fact fully attested by a review of the pastoral industry of the Colony during the last ten years. The Auditor-General of the Colony, in a paper read before the Royal Society in December, 1872, says :—

The statistics show that we commenced the decennial period with the following live stock, namely :—

Horses.	Cattle.	Sheep.
273,389	2,620,383	6,145,651

and that we close the decennary with

| 304,100 | 2,014,888 | 16,278,697 |

that is to say, we have increased our horse stock by over 30,000; we are poorer in horned cattle by over 600,000, and we have increased our sheep by over 10,000,000.

This is a striking result, and one which can hardly have been anticipated, viz., that, whilst we have increased our flocks in the ten years 165 per cent., we have lost 23 per cent. of our herds.

Between 1862 and 1871—omitting the two years 1867 and 1868, in which no statistics of the "overland" traffic were taken—the exports and imports of cattle and sheep across the border to Victoria stood thus, viz.:—

	Cattle.	Sheep.
Exports ...	551,464	3,440,790
Imports ...	33,834	195,213
Net exports in the 8 years...	517,630	3,245,577

The tables of the Registrar General, which exhibit the export of wool—the produce of the Colony—furnish the following information:—They show us that in the year 1862 our flocks produced 20,988,393 lbs. of wool, of the estimated value of £1,801,186, which gives an average of over 3 lbs. 6 ozs. per sheep, and an estimated value of nearly one shilling and ninepence per pound. In 1866 the production had increased to 36,980,685 lbs. of wool, with an estimated value of £2,830,348, or a little over one shilling and six-pence per pound; thus exhibiting an increase in the production to the extent of 76 per cent. Whilst in the last five years of the series—that is, in the year 1871—the exports reached the highest figures ever sent away, namely, 65,611,953 lbs. of wool, and the estimated value of £4,748,160, or a little over one shilling and fivepence per pound. Not far short of five millions sterling, and equal to an increase of production of 212 per cent. in ten years, and nearly 80 per cent. in the last five years. The clip of 1871 gave an average yield of four pounds per sheep, that is, ten ounces over the clip of 1862, owing probably in great measure to the larger proportion of wool going home in grease. We have no means of ascertaining the actual return proceeds of the clip of last year; indeed it cannot yet have been all realized. I shall not be accused of overstating the case, however, if I put down the surplus return to the Colony, over and above the value before stated, at a million and a half sterling, thus bringing up the value of the clip to six millions and a quarter sterling.

We have no means of ascertaining the value of the home consumption; we must therefore be content to estimate the production by the value of the exports as expressed in the returns before us.

I find, then, that we exported seaward last year, the produce of own flocks and herds, to the value of—

Live stock	£441,330
Salt and preserved meats	133,226
Hides and skins	48,283
Tallow	245,727
Total	£468,566

Thus bringing up the value of our pastoral produce to a sum approaching seven millions sterling.

But these figures include the value of the live stock, wool and tallow, exported "overland." I must therefore, to make the comparison complete, look up the value of the pastoral produce so exported last year. I find it is as follows, viz. :—

Live stock	£914,893
Tallow, skins, &c.	23,594
Wool	2,443,380
Total	£3,381,867

If we add this to the amount previously estimated, we shall arrive at an aggregate sum exceeding eight millions and a half sterling as the total estimated value of our pastoral exports for the year 1871, viz. :—

Wool, seaward	£4,748,160
Tallow, &c., ditto	468,606
Wool, live stock, tallow, &c., overland	3,381,867
Grand Total	£8,598,633

V.—MINERAL WEALTH.

Late discoveries have shown that much of the granite soil of the country, long regarded as worthless for agriculture, is rich in tin and gold, so that there is now hardly any portion of the territory which cannot be made tributary to the wealth or sustenance of the people. The Mineral Map which accompanies this pamphlet is designed to show the metalliferous deposits of the Country; and, with the addition of the other principal minerals, namely coal, kerosene, and precious stones, gives a catalogue of all that is at present known respecting the depositions of gold, silver, copper, iron, tin, diamonds, and other gems. What is known of the vast extent, variety, and richness of our mineral lands is the more remarkable, seeing that all search in this department has been left to private enterprise and that investigation by the Government has yet to begin. In the smaller Colonies of the group geological surveys have been completed; and when it becomes practicable to perform a similar service for New South Wales, it is by no means improbable that much larger areas and more valuable mines than any yet discovered will be made known.

Gold Discovery.

Gold in Australia was first discovered in New South Wales, and the actual search for the precious metal was commenced, in 1851, in the Western Districts of the Colony. Seven years before that, however, Sir R. I. Murchison, without ever having been in Australia, predicted that gold would be found in the mountain chains which run from north to south of the Colony; and he went so far as to recommend the unemployed miners of Cornwall to come out here and dig for it. Similar prognostications were made about the same time by the Rev. W. B. Clarke, the eminent geologist, who has resided in Sydney for many years. The discovery made at Ophir led to the finding of gold in the soil and rocks of the Colony over tracts many miles in extent. It was quickly ascertained that the country drained by the Macquarie, the Turon, the Abercrombie, and the Meroo, and more recently that watered by the Lachlan, the Darling, the Murrumbidgee, the Cudgegong, the Shoalhaven, and the Clarence, was all auriferous. It is thought that mineral discovery in New South Wales, notwithstanding that so much has been accomplished during the last twenty years, is still in its infancy. The proclaimed Gold Fields, extending with short intervals the entire length of the Country, and westward about 200 miles from the coast, comprise an area of about 13,656 square miles, and number more than eighty distinct fields. The richest of these are on the western side of the Great Dividing Range. They are shown on the map by a yellow tint, and auriferous lands unproclaimed as far as yet known by yellow dots. It will be seen that there is hardly a district in the Colony that has not been invaded by the digger and made to contribute to the gold currency of the World. Gold has been found in the gizzards of fowls, and picked up in the streets of Bathurst. It has been brought up from the bottom of the sea, off Port Macquarie, by the sounding line of H.M.S. "Herald"; it is distributed amongst the sands of the Shoalhaven shore, and it glitters among the pebbles which are strewn along the beach at the Richmond, so that gold may be said to gild our whole Pacific coast; and it is the opinion of men best informed on the subject that there are vast treasures of the precious metal in the alluvial lands along the remote western boundary of the Colony yet untouched.

Gold in the Soil.

The "Alluvial" Gold Fields, as they are termed, commonly occur along the beds of rivers, where the gold washed down from the hills has been deposited. The auriferous soil in many places is found on the surface, more particularly in the bends or beds of a watercourse, where, from its specific gravity, the gold has settled;

and where the deposits are deep, the soil has paid for washing from a depth of one to thirty feet. At Gulgong, the miners have sunk through a thick belt of basaltic rock, and have come upon an ancient watercourse, where the underlying wash-dirt has richly rewarded their long and patient toil. Similar deposits of gold have been found at many other places.

Alluvial mining, however, has not generally been carried on with much system or steady application. The diggers, inflamed by reports of enormous yields, have too often abandoned payable fields for others not more remunerative, and they have thus squandered much of their energy and earnings upon toilsome journeys in pursuit of dazzling fortunes. But a portion of the digging population has displayed great industry, perseverance, and intelligence in mining operations. The diggers have cut working races for miles in length, round the hills, and bringing the water on to fields by methods most ingenious; and, by association, have often gained all the advantages of capital. In periods of dry weather, the beds of rivers and creeks have yielded much treasure, and, in times of heavy rain, when the watercourses have become swollen, the miners have had to betake themselves to the high grounds, which the increased supply of water has brought under profitable work. Large sluicing Companies have, within the last few years, been formed, and operations on the high lands are now likely to be more systematically carried on. At Araluen, the surface soil is stripped down to the wash-dirt, a depth of about twenty feet, and the stripping carted away to some other spot. The underlying auriferous soil is then carefully collected and washed down to the bed rock. The claims are generally worked by ten or a dozen men, and pumping-engines are employed to keep them clear of water. It is not within the scope of this paper to relate instances of individual success; for a catalogue which should include all the large finds of lucky diggers in New South Wales would be more bulky than this pamphlet itself. If space permitted, it would not be difficult to shew that the Alluvial Gold Fields of New South Wales have been, and still are, as rich as any in the World.

GOLD IN THE ROCK.

Systematic mining for gold in the rock is comparatively new in New South Wales. It marks an era in the Colony's progress, and the last two years' work has produced results which are without a parallel in the history of this or any other gold producing country. The existence of gold in our mountain ranges has long been known to miners, and yet, strange as it must appear, nearly every discovery has been the result of accident. Thus, for instance, an aboriginal, in the year of the gold discovery, saw a glittering mass on the side of a mountain on the Meroo. He told his master, Dr. Kerr, who knocked off two or three hundredweight of rock, from which was extracted a hundredweight of gold. The site of the rich mines on Hawkins' Hill had attention drawn to them in a similar way. A miner, named Adams, weary in his search after horses, sat down to rest, and by mere accident knocked off a piece of rock, the glittering specks in which revealed the presence of hidden treasure. That rugged hill, rising to a height of nearly two thousand feet above the waters of the Turon, which flows past its foot, has now been found to be reticulated with auriferous quartz veins, and well deserves the name of the Golden Mountain. It is the centre of a region of gold-bearing quartz reefs, which run for many miles to the north and the south of it, and around its summit a population of several thousand souls has permanently settled. From two of the mines on that Hill, during the last six months of 1872, gold to the value of £162,850, after paying escort fees and Mint charges, was obtained. Let one more illustration from a different part of the Colony, suffice. We take it from the report of the Royal Commission:—

O'Brien's Reef, at Grenfell, was, to all appearance on the surface, some five years ago, much the same as the dozens of reefs that are to be passed over in a day's ride in most of the Southern and Western Districts. No indications of its auriferous character appeared to exist to the eye of the ordinary traveller, or even to the practical miner. A shepherd, in the employ of a squatter in the neighbourhood, in an idle moment broke some pieces of the stone, and saw a small speck of gold in them. He and some four or five miners opened up the reef in the latter end of 1866, taking up as a claim six men's ground, or 180 feet. From that time to the present, the claimholders have raised and crushed 14,673 tons of stone, which have yielded 16,481 ounces of gold, or at the rate of 1 oz. 3 dwts. to the ton. The cost of raising and crushing the stone, including all expenses, is estimated by the shareholders at about 20s. per ton. The value of the gold produced would be about £60,000, and thus the profits on this one small claim in five years would be, in round numbers, £45,000. But this was not all that resulted from the accidental circumstance of the discovery of a small speck of gold in a by no means very promising looking reef, by the shepherd. Other reefs were tested adjoining the one we have spoken of, and indeed the discovery and working of the Emu Creek Gold Field took place. From October, 1866, the time of the discovery, to the 30th September, 1871, that Field has sent to Sydney, by escort, the large quantity of 182,061 ounces of gold, of the value of £723,642.

Quartz reefs have, within the last two years, been found side by side with the alluvial diggings in every part of the Colony, and a large amount of capital has now been attracted to them. Last year 5,350 acres of quartz reefs were taken up under lease in the Northern District; 21,363 acres in the Western District; and 3,155 acres in the Southern District—the total for the whole Colony taken up during 1872 being just upon 30,000 acres. Sufficient time has not elapsed to enable many of the mines which have lately been started to become productive, for sometimes the miner has to sink through two or three hundred feet of hard rock before he strikes the reef at a depth which he thinks will pay him to raise stone for crushing. There is one reef in the Colony about eight feet wide, but the average width of the gold-bearing stone would not be more than from one to three feet. Some of the richest mines have obtained much of their gold from veins less than a foot in width.

At present it is difficult to speak with accuracy of the productive character or otherwise of the quartz reefs of the Colony, for there is no Department for Mines where results are collected and compared. There can be little doubt, however, that the auriferous rocks of New South Wales are much richer than any which have yet been discovered in other Countries; and it is the generally received opinion of practical miners that longer experience will still more clearly demonstrate the fact. In the neighbouring Colony of Victoria, Companies are, in many instances, working reefs which only give such small returns as from 4 to 5 dwts. to the ton. Mining and engineering skill, and large and powerful machinery are brought to bear on such reefs, and, as a rule, the dividends and yields give a handsome return for the investment of the capital.

The Press of this Colony contains many statements, showing the rate per ton of quartz crushed, the average of some being little short of 1,000 ozs. to the ton. But many of these statements may emanate from interested speculators, and it is prudent to regard them with caution. The only satisfactory test of the value of a quartz reef is to be found in the result, not of trial crushings, but of practical work extending over a period of months.

The following returns of the work done at three of the quartz crushing machines in the Tambaroora district, taken from a local paper, are, however, definite, and no doubt trustworthy:—

The quantities of stone crushed at Pullen and Rawthorne's battery, and the yield per ton were as below:—Scandinavian, 85 tons, 1 oz. 3 dwts.; ditto, 79 tons, 1 oz. 4 dwts.; ditto, 89 tons, 17½ dwts.; Rawsthorne's, 304 tons, 4 ozs. 10 dwts.; ditto, 306 tons, 4 ozs. 12 dwts.; ditto, 302 tons, 1 oz. 1 dwt.;. Beyers and Holterman, 108 tons, 13 ozs.; ditto, 148 tons, 5 ozs. 8 dwts.; ditto, 264 tons, 8 ozs.; ditto, 9 tons, 1,500 ozs.; Paxton and Co., 399 tons, 4 ozs.; ditto, 366 tons, not reported; All Nations, 21 tons, 5 ozs.; Henry Hotston, 1½ ton, 1 oz. 3 dwts.; Oxon and Co., 4 tons, 5 dwts.; Frenchman's, 30 tons, 1 oz. 17 dwts.; Creighton and Beard's, 187 tons, 3 ozs. 14½ dwts.; ditto, 198 tons, 5 ozs. 10 dwts.; Herman's, 57½ tons, 3 ozs. 8 dwts.; Black Watch, G. Gully, 27 tons, 7 dwts. The undermentioned claims crushed at Vickery's battery:—Frenchman's, Rampant Lion, Fischer and Beard's, All Nations, Beard and Tallentire's, Cosmopolitan, and Paxton and Co. The quantity crushed for them was 3,263 tons, which ran from 8 dwts. to 17 ozs. of gold to the ton. Chappell's battery has crushed 4,000 tons of quartz, which yielded 40,000 ozs. of gold from the following claims:—Krohmann's (which contributed the largest portion), Carroll and Beard's, Marshall's, Brown's, Cock, Atwood, and Dwyer's, Star of Peace, Frenchman's, and Canton Lead; total average 10 ozs. to the ton.

The richest mines yet opened are those known as Krohmann's and Beyers and Holterman's. We have long been accustomed to speak of potatoes, sugar, flour, and other commodities by the cwt., but it is comparatively a new thing to regard gold in that wholesale light. Now, however, on five or six occasions gold has been blasted out of the rock by the hundredweight at a time, and we are becoming more familiar with the idea. The following statements of results of less than a year's work in Krohmann's and Beyers and Holterman's mines have been furnished to the compiler of this pamphlet by the Manager of those Companies:—

KROHMANN'S Co.		BEYERS AND HOLTERMAN'S Co.	
Stone.	Produce of gold.	Stone.	Produce of gold.
	ozs.		ozs.
Weight not taken	5,981· 0	142 tons	768·82
2 cwt.	812·28	273 „	15,510·81
15 tons 7 „	6,989·13		
165 „ 0 „	835·46	415 „	16,279·63 ozs.
71 „ 0 „	470·05		
185 „ 0 „	8,982·36	Net proceeds as per Mint returns	£63,224 12s.
436 „ 9 „	24,079 ozs. 8 dwts.		
Net proceeds as per Mint returns	£93,616 11s. 9d.		

From each of those mines gold to the value of many thousand pounds was taken before they passed into the hands of joint stock companies, which was about the middle of 1872.

Since these facts were obtained, other stupendous yields have been reported. The *Empire's* telegram from Hill End, dated February 1, 1873, says: " Beyers and Holterman have raised one hundredweight gold in two hundredweight of stuff, to-day. Expect to shoot out monster specimen, with at least two hundredweight of gold, on Monday." It is not a matter of wonder that mining industry in the Colony should be greatly stimulated by results so marvellous. In respect of one of the yields included in the foregoing statement, the mining correspondent of the *Sydney Morning Herald* sends the following information:—" On Friday night last, the largest and richest specimen this colony has produced, I suppose, was taken from the claim of Beyers and Holterman. It is really a wonderful one—a slab of gold. Its weight is about 6½ cwt.; and I believe I am within the mark in saying that there are 2 cwt. of gold in it. I went, together with nearly the whole town, to look at it. The claim was like a fair, and a regular stream of people threaded the steep packing tracks leading down to it. It was hung up for exhibition, and during the day hundreds, including many of the fair sex, went down to see it. At the same time that I went to look at this, Mr. Bullock, the manager, kindly revealed the treasures of the iron box, in which are specimens, not so large certainly, but prettier to look upon. The monster is not alone in his glory; he has fellows bigger and richer below, I am told. He appears to form part of a lode rather than a vein, as no quartz seems to be showing— nothing but mundic and a slate casing." In a subsequent communication he again wrote respecting this claim:—" The all-absorbing topic of conversation is the result of Beyers and Holterman's crushing. The amount of amalgam hard squeezed, and probably nearly two-thirds gold, is about 8 cwt., irrespective of the monster specimen and those raised since its appearance. About 6 cwt. of amalgam is being retorted, leaving 2 cwt. to be operated on. The nugget goes through to-morrow, and a considerable quantity of stone, together with specimens, remains to go through. On Wednesday I went over the claim to see principally what was to come, as there was talk of another monster bigger than the first, and certainly there was every reason to expect one; over seven feet of what looked like a bar of gold lay glittering along the stope. On Friday this was taken down, but broke in the operation: so that, although extremely rich, it did not equal its predecessor in size. Gold can be seen all through the claim, and another cross-cut at a level considerably below the present rich workings, put through them to the west, has discovered another batch of veins calculated to go 6 ozs. to the ton. The wealth of the claim is great, and requires to be seen to be believed."

The same correspondent, writing of Beyers and Holterman's claim from Hill End, on the 3rd February, 1873, says:—

Day after day brings the same news. More rich specimens! I went down to the claim this morning, and arrived just in time to see a monster landed, that probably eclipses all that has been produced anywhere. The fellow that caused such excitement last crushing was but a child to this. It can't be far short of half a ton in weight, and as for the gold in it no one would venture to say how much there is. Gold seems as plentiful in the claim as fruit in a rich plum pudding.

The *Herald's* telegram, two days later, reports: "22½ tons of stone crushed from Carroll & Board's claim yielded 1,567 ozs. of gold, and more is to come." On the 25th of the same month, the mining article of the same journal contains the following statement:—

A supplementary crushing of 52 cwt. of stone from Carroll & Beard's mine has yielded 758 ozs. Krohmann's crushing of 139 tons gave 14,067 ozs. of gold, and about 350 more are expected from specimens and tailings. A dividend of 12s. 6d. per share has been declared. £2,000 has been added to reserve fund, and about £3,400 set aside for current expenses until next crushing. This Company was formed in May last, with a capital of £80,000 in £1 shares. The crushings since that date have yielded nearly 38,500 ounces of gold, valued at £148,674.' The dividends declared amount to £1 13s. per share. Beyers & Holterman's crushing of 324¼ tons has given a total yield of 4,577 ounces.

One result of the sudden development of our quartz mines has been, that unscrupulous speculators have traded on the credulity of the community, and companies have been formed by the dozen, involving a capital of many thousand pounds without any inquiry having been made as to whether the ground really contained a quartz vein at all. This ill-considered precipitation will probably operate as a serious check to mining enterprize; but, no one who makes fair inquiry can avoid the conclusion that gold mining in New South Wales is one of the most promising fields for the investment of capital to be found.

The area is practically unlimited, and the risks are not excessive. The value of our quartz mines to the man whose labour is his only capital, is this, that they give constant work and good wages.

The Miner in New South Wales.

Untravelled dwellers in other lands are perhaps not prepared to hear that the gold miner in Australia is not a ruffian armed with bowie knife and revolver, but as peaceable, well-disposed, and industrious as the average run of men in the oldest settled communities in the world. He is far above the agricultural labourer of Europe in the scale of intelligence, for his wits are sharpened by travel, and his life produces a stalwart form and a manly self-reliant character. He is addicted to reading newspapers, and his principal failings are a fondness for the pipe and a propensity to lecture Members of Parliament. A mining community, for the first few months of its existence, has not a very prepossessing appearance. Mounds of earth and masses of building material are strewn about, and the huts and tents of the miners are of the roughest description. An orderly township, however, is quickly established, with stores in which every commodity can be bought at reasonable rates. Side by side with these are found Public Schools, commodious, well-built, and well-ventilated, whose walls are hung with maps and pictures, and which are furnished in a style equal if not superior to any of the common schools of Great Britain. Almost simultaneously with the schools come the churches, and these are commonly built after models to be found in the towns and villages all over England.

All the great gold fields of the west are within two days' journey of the capital, and there is not a gold field or mining settlement to be found in all the land which, however remote, cannot be reached from Sydney, either by railway, steam-ship, or mail-coach, in less than a week. Twenty years ago there were neither roads nor bridges worthy of the name, and the man who penetrated the trackless wilds of the Australian forest, stood a fair chance of being drowned in the rivers, or of being hopelessly lost in the bush. If he reached his destination, he found that the prices of provisions of all kinds were enormously high, and perhaps beyond the power of his purse to obtain. Now, however, gold mining is one of the settled industries of the country. The miner can live as cheaply on the gold fields as the artisan in the city, and his life and his property are as secure as they could be in the most orderly township of Britain. During the last two years there have been migrations of population to the extent of from eight to twenty thousand souls attracted from all parts of Australia, from New Zealand and other countries beyond the sea, to our gold fields in the west, and our tin mines in the north, and yet not a single instance of disorder has occurred. It is seldom that more than one or two constables are stationed even on the largest fields (although by means of the telegraph a force could be concentrated at any point within a few hours); the new comers are perfect strangers one to the other, and yet, such is the respect of the people for constituted authority, and their regard, each for the rights of others, that no serious disturbance is ever apprehended.

No special skill beyond that which any one who can handle a pick and shovel will quickly acquire is requisite to enable a man to become a gold-digger; and all the implements required can either be made by the man himself or bought for a few pounds. The regulations of the Government are conceived in the most liberal spirit, and while they protect the miner to the fullest possible extent, they at the same time ensure the freest scope to his industry. The gold in the soil is, of course, the property of the Crown; and before any man can take it he must get what is called a "miner's right." This authority to dig or mine for gold is given to all who apply for it. It costs ten shillings a year, and entitles its possessor to take up ground upon any gold field to the extent of from 60 feet by 60 feet to 114 feet by 114 feet, according to the class of mining pursued upon the particular field. If a man wants to open a quartz mine he can take up fifty feet along the line of reef, with a breadth of 100 yards on each side. His miner's right also entitles him to occupy half an acre of land for his dwelling upon any proclaimed gold field, and to vote for the election of a Member of Parliament. All these privileges any man may enjoy in New South Wales for 10s. a year—the price of a day's work. But the miner is not restricted to one claim; he can take up a hundred if he likes, by virtue of his right; but then he must keep men at work upon them, and every man he so employs must also have the "right." This is not all. The miner can take up sluicing claims to the extent of ten acres; and if this be too circumscribed an area he may by the payment of £1 per acre per annum take out a lease of alluvial or quartz ground for any number of acres not exceeding twenty-five in one block (and as many twenty-five acre blocks as he pleases), or of river beds to the extent of 1,000 yards, on payment of a yearly rental of £1 for every 100 yards so taken up. To prevent monopoly, however, and to protect the interests of the miners as a body as well as of the State, the Regulations provide that the miner shall forfeit his claim or his lease if he fail to work it. There is an export duty on gold of 1s. 3d. per oz.

Persevering industry is the great essential to success; but the more sound sense is brought to bear upon the pursuit the greater will be the reward. The prospects of the digger were never brighter than at present. He is his own master, and he enjoys an amount of robust health, freedom, and sturdy independence such as falls to the lot of few manual labourers in other lands. He has in New South Wales the certainty of earning a good livelihood, with the chance of making a fortune. As for the quartz miner his position is this: He works eight hours a day for five days a week, and four hours on Saturday. He is paid £2 10s. to £3 a week; and if at that rate he thinks he is not earning enough, why, then, all he has to do is to mark out a claim for himself and begin work on his own account. Some of the mines are now worth two or three hundred thousand pounds, and were a few years ago taken up by one or two poor men in virtue of their miners' rights.

This remark applies to those claims which have been mentioned in this chapter; and one or two other instances by way of illustration may suffice. "J.H., a native of Sydney, went to Tambaroora a few years since, and had only £5 in his pocket. On his arrival he worked on the several reefs of the district with varied success, sometimes almost beaten but never despairing. When fortune failed him as a principal he turned to again as a miner, and by his steady conduct and regular habits could always manage to put by a few pounds, with which once more to make a fresh start on his own account. By the advice and pecuniary help of a friend he bought half a claim, then known as the "A 1." For eighteen months before the claim had been worked with no good result, but after eight months more of continuous labour the gold was struck. When down the shaft one night he picked up a capful of quartz worth £20, and that insignificant sum was the precursor of enormous yields. In less than two months from that time, J.H. and his mate cleared more than £8,000, and long after that the mine continued to yield them quarterly dividends of £5,000 per man. J.H. retired from actual work, and sold his half of the mine for £12,000; but the buyer was unable to complete the purchase, and the claim was withdrawn. The very next crushing yielded a clear dividend of £10,000, and the next two gave a clear profit of £700 each. Once more the claim was offered, and was quickly bought up by the public for £33,000, the amount being subscribed in £1 shares. At the time of writing this, the shares are at a premium of 11s., and are expected soon to be worth £2 apiece. J.H. has acquired considerable influence in the localities where he has lived, and, as a temperance reformer, has induced many hundreds of the digging population to become total abstainers. He now resides in an elegant mansion overlooking one of the picturesque bays of Sydney Harbour, and represents an important constituency in the Parliament of the Country." J.P. is another miner of a similar stamp, who has not been less successful. The compiler of this pamphlet visited the mine which bears his name, in May last (1872), and in a description of the workings furnished to one of the metropolitan journals, gave the following information which he derived from the manager:—" The mine consists of eight men's ground, and has a frontage of 122 feet 6 inches along the line of reef, with a depth of 300 yards. It was taken up in 1866, and the workings date from early in the next year, the first crushing being had some thirteen months later. About twelve months ago, one of the five shares into which the claim was then divided sold for £4,000, or at the rate of £20,000 for the whole. A few weeks since, however, the claim passed into the hands of the present Company for £160,000. £40,000 was taken out of the claim last year, and £30,000 has already been realized this year. One crushing, the proceeds of the first eight weeks' work in this year, yielded 7,103 ounces of gold from 268½ tons of quartz, giving a dividend of £4,800 on each of the five shares then held, after paying working expenses. Thirty-eight men are employed in this claim, working in day and night shifts." J.P., who was, and perhaps still is, one of the largest owners in the mine, is now a resident in one of the suburbs of the capital; and he bids fair to achieve a reputation as a philanthropist more enduring than that which he has acquired as a gold miner.

GOLD PRODUCTION AND PROSPECTS.

Gold and other mining has latterly received a great impetus in New South Wales; and the Census of 1871 shewed that we had 18,529 miners in the Colony; and of these, more than 16,000 were engaged in gold-mining. The increase in the number of miners has been almost exclusively in gold-mining, and the number now so employed is far greater than at any former time. During the last twenty-two years New South Wales has exported gold to the value of £40,095,823, and nearly the whole of that large quantity has been washed from the soil by rough and wasteful processes. The extent of gold-bearing land held under lease to the end of 1872 was 31,895 acres of alluvial, 31,941 acres of quartz, and 184,700 yards of river beds. Nearly the whole of the quartz leases were taken out in 1872 ; and they are granted on such terms that the lessee is practically in the position of a freeholder, so long as he complies with the conditions, which require that he shall work the ground.

The auriferous wealth of this Colony should have a special personal interest to the intending emigrant, for the demands which the mining community make upon the whole Colony for farm produce, food supplies, clothing, and machinery, vitalises every industry we have. If any should suppose that the gold-bearing lands of New South Wales are, like those of many other Countries, all occupied, that, we may tell him, is quite a mistake. The Gold Fields Royal Commission of Inquiry, consisting of gentlemen of great mining and engineering experience, visited all the Gold Fields of the Colony in 1870, and examined witnesses wherever they went. In their Report to the Government, published in 1871, they say :—

A very strong impression exists on our minds, as a result of this examination, that the resources of New South Wales, both in its auriferous treasures and its other mineral riches, have been very much underrated and undervalued. As regards the gold mines, we have seen a great many old and partially abandoned Gold Fields, in which it is evident vast quantities of gold yet remain to be unearthed. The individual miner, working chiefly as he has hitherto, merely with his pick and shovel, has no doubt exhausted the ground of nearly all the gold that, by the aid only of such appliances, he could extract ; but there yet remains on such old diggings a vast field for enterprise, when he shall be assisted by associated capital and by efficient machinery. Very wet ground, both alluvial and quartz, as also surface hills and the beds of rivers and creeks, are to be found in a great number of places, which, although known to be payable and indeed in much of it known to be rich, remain at the present time undeveloped and unworked. The reason of this is chiefly that the individual miner, however suitable he may be to prospect, and, in most instances, to efficiently develop new auriferous ground, has not generally the means for such extensive undertakings and works as are required to extract the precious metal in payable quantities, where the ground on which he operates has been previously worked, and the cream, so to speak, taken from it. The introduction on old or partially worked ground of costly pumping machinery to keep wet claims dry, extensive races or watercourses to bring water to arid ground, and machinery for hauling, crushing, and puddling, would, in a great number of instances, if available to the practical miner, vastly tend to increase our national wealth, and give employment to a greatly increased population. From the rough and imperfect mode in which the gold mines of the country have hitherto been worked (partly attributable to new rushes taking the miners away from their claims before they had been thoroughly tried, and partly to the want at the time of knowledge of mining and the absence of proper appliances), there are great quantities of old workings which will, we believe, yield a rich harvest when the capitalist can be enticed to lend his helping hand to their development.

In what may be termed new or unprospected ground, our observations induce to the belief that a very large field for enterprise and the use of capital also exists. Gold-mining on a large scale may really be said to be only just commencing in New South Wales, more particularly the branch of it known as quartz-mining. There appears to have been, and indeed to be now, to some extent, an opinion that gold-mining must, from its very nature, be merely ephemeral; that, unlike most other occupations, and indeed other kinds of mining, gold-digging cannot last in the Country for any length of time. The shallow and easily worked diggings, discovered in the early days of the gold discovery, greatly induced this belief, and did much to retard the advancement of the gold-mining interest. Of late, however, deep alluvial leads and rich quartz reefs have come to be worked, which are fast leading to the impression that very many gold mines will, like many tin and copper mines, be worked for many years—it may be for centuries. The idea that quartz reefs ceased to be auriferous at a hundred feet or two beneath the surface, is quite exploded. In this Colony, as for instance, at Grenfell, Tambaroora, and Adelong, a depth of 300 feet and over has been reached, and at that depth as good stone obtained as at the surface. In Victoria, 800 feet has been reached in reefs which are yielding rich stone; and in California we hear of reefs being profitably worked at 1,000 and 1,100 feet beneath the surface. It is impossible to say to what extent reefing, as it is called, may be developed in New South Wales. The country is in many auriferous regions literally covered with auriferous reefs, not rich enough, it may be, on the surface, to tempt the individual miner or the promoters of Companies to attempt to work them under the present state of things, but which are yet, many of them, destined, we believe, to yield remunerative occupation to a large population, and employment to much capital.

It is the opinion of many competent witnesses who came before us, that there are immense tracts of country in the Colony which have every indication of being auriferous, but which have as yet not been at all prospected. We concur in the view which is prevalent amongst the gold-miners, that it is highly probable that rich and extensive gold fields will be discovered for many years to come; and that the few diggings hitherto worked are but a very small part of the gold mines which are destined to enrich the people of this Country. Mr. Emmett, a gentleman of large experience in gold-mining affairs, particularly in Victoria, one of the witnesses whom we examined, upon being interrogated as to his opinion of the mineral resources of New South Wales, says:—"I consider the auriferous districts of New South Wales far larger than those of any other Australian Colony, and as rich." So also Mr. Travers Jones, the Manager of a Mining Company in this Colony, and a gentleman who for years has been engaged in various mining undertakings both in Victoria, New Zealand, and New South Wales, says:—"There is already a very large extent of known auriferous country throughout those parts of the Colony which I have specified as having been under my own personal observation, which would furnish scope for remunerative operations for generations to come." Mr. James H. Griffin—a gentleman who has been a Gold Commissioner in the Colony, and who at the time of his examination by us was Manager of a Mining Company—bears testimony also to the abundant mineral treasures this country possesses. He says:—"I believe that, at all events as far as the Braidwood District is concerned, the auriferous resources of the Colony are unsurpassed. There are other indications of mineral riches; both lead and copper have been discovered; precious stones have also been found.

To this testimony we will only add that of the Rev. W. B. Clarke, M.A., F.G.S., F.R.G.S. That distinguished geologist delivered an Address before the Royal Society of New South Wales, on the 22nd of May, 1872, from which we extract the paragraphs subjoined:—

Now and then we hear of fresh alluvial diggings, such, for instance, as those at Gulgong, which are in an extension of a field proclaimed many years since; but experience has shown that an increased and iucreasing resort to the crushing-mill is influencing the minds of the mining community.

That gold production is on the increase no one can doubt; and if prospectors will but go out into districts that abound not far from the vicinity even of gold fields, where no pick or spade has been employed, new ground will assuredly be found where "reefs," as they are called, meet the eye of the traveller at almost every turn, and where there is every legitimate reason to infer that some will be productive.

It is not too much to say that no sooner are we off the carboniferous areas rich in coal and its associated minerals, than we are in a region in which are tracts where gold and copper and lead abound. And, passing from the sedimentary to the plutonic rocks, we can discover granites which, however barren externally, are within frequently charged with the valuable ore of tin. So that the three great geological divisions of our Colony are replete with mineral treasures that are practically inexhaustible.

It is, perhaps, difficult to assign any strict measurement in superficial area to the actual amount of land capable of furnishing present proofs of this, because, as we well know, metals are local, and not universal.

During my last visits to different parts of the Western District, I not only saw the operations that are going on, but passed over many miles of country in which the rocks that belong to a golden area yet remain in their original condition, and will so remain till some fortunate adventurer stumbles by accident on a tangible encouragement.

Coal.

The coal measures of New South Wales are most extensive and valuable. They extend from the 29th to the 35th parallel of S. latitude; they crop out to the water's edge along many miles of the seaboard, and vast carboniferous areas are intersected by two lines of railway at distances of nearly 100 miles from the metropolis, while the third line, that to the north, runs through coal fields over nearly its whole length. The New South Wales coal is admirably adapted for steam purposes. It is burnt in all the steamships trading to the southern hemisphere; and meets the English coal in the markets of India and China at equal prices. The Imperial Government have issued instructions to the effect that the squadrons of the British Navy stationed in the Pacific shall henceforth be supplied with Australian coal; and instructions from the Admiralty have been received authorizing the purchase of 11,000 tons of New South Wales coal, to be delivered during the present year at the various naval stations in the Indian and China Seas. The only limit to our export trade in this commodity is that imposed by the tonnage of vessels seeking freights. The principal collieries at present worked are situated within 10 miles of Newcastle, a commodious harbour about 50 miles north of Sydney; but valuable mines are also worked near Wollongong, 60 miles south of Sydney, and at Hartley, about 90 miles inland on the western line of railway. The A. A. Co.'s seam is 163 feet from the surface, and 150 feet below sea level, and its average thickness is about ten feet. It is highly bituminous; and may be taken as an illustration of several other seams in the same locality which are however nearer the surface. Preparations are being made to work a seam near Murrurundi, 120 miles north-west of Newcastle; and efforts are also being made to bring the coal of the Clarence into the local market. A large area of our coal fields must long remain undeveloped excepting for local requirements, for it is not likely that mines far inland will ever be able to compete with those only a few miles from the ports of shipment. At Stroud a seam of more than 30 feet in thickness crops out on the banks of a creek, and this thickness has been verified by several trial pits sunk in the dip side. Another seam near Branxton, on the northern line of railway, is 22 feet thick, and contains no less than seven varieties of coal, all of them good and separated only by thin partings of shale. The late Mr. Wm. Keene, Examiner for Coal Fields, in a report to the Government, says: "I have examined seams more than 700 miles to the north of Newcastle, belonging to the same deposits as we are working in the Hunter, covered and underlaid by the same fossil flora and fauna; and we may without boasting claim to rank with the most extensive coal fields in the world." Locomotive power is used at all the Hunter River mines, and, with the shipping facilities which exist at Newcastle at the present time, we are able to load 40,000 tons of coal per week. The means of shipment can of course be indefinitely increased.

The Hartley coal measures are the last which have been brought under tribute by the miner, and in a year or two their trade with the western interior must become very great. The coal measures there are close to the railway, and they are known to crop out over an area of 10 square miles. The seams are from 9 to 11 feet thick, and the coal is used by the locomotives on the Government railway. The area under lease for coal mining up to the end of 1872 was 34,720 acres; and the number of coal miners 2,150. The prices of coal at Newcastle free on board ship are: best screened, 12s.; unscreened, 11s.; small, 6s. The miners are paid 4s. 3d. per ton for hewing coal. The miners work by the piece and can therefore get much or little as pleases them. They seldom work more than eight hours, and in that time can average *three* tons. The work, however, is not always continuous as the demand is sometimes slack, and then there is no work for the "back shift."

The quantity of coal raised from New South Wales Mines to the end of 1871, was 9,816,693 tons; the quantity exported was 5,885,493 tons, of the value of £3,790,223.

Our coal has established a high reputation in all the countries with which we trade. In 1871 (the last year for which returns are available) we exported 565,429 tons of the value of £256,690.

Victoria took 84,916 tons; New Zealand 39,705; Queensland 1,694; Western Australia 390; South Australia 29,786; Tasmania 5,979; South Sea Islands 1,804; New Caledonia 149; Shanghai 12,703; United States (California) 24,814; Hongkong 23,211; Petropaulouski 4,542; Mauritius 2,962; Foo Chow Foo 558; Manila 3,431; Valparaiso 203; Singapore 1,474; Bombay 4,016; Japan 948; Choo Foo 378; Calcutta 1,722; Ilo Ilo 152; Java 3,568; Honolulu 3,592; Bankok 134; Amoy 950; Ceylon 1,380; Guam 161; Saigon 412; Sumatra 466; and Moluccas 490.

His Excellency Sir Hercules Robinson visited Newcastle and the Hunter in September of last year; and at a banquet given by the citizens in his honor, he made the following remarks, which are valuable, not merely for the information they contain, but as conveying the impressions of a gentleman of large experience and wide observation in other parts of the world, who had then recently assumed the office of Governor-in-Chief of this Colony. He said:—

I believe this extensive district is second to none in the Colony as regards the wealth of its resources, and the enterprising and industrious character of its population. Nor are its resources a matter of merely local interest. For in its almost unlimited coal-fields it appears to me that the district possesses a permanent source of wealth, which not only must enrich this immediate locality, but which will, I believe, contribute more than any other of the rich and varied productions of this wonderful country to establish the future greatness of New South Wales upon a solid basis. The effect which this important industry has had upon the trade and prosperity of Newcastle in the last few years has been very remarkable. I believe it is only fifty years since a gentleman, now residing amongst you, and whose son, I am told, is present here to-day, embarked in what must have been then considered an undertaking of a very speculative character, in asking permission from the Government to build a sloop of fifty tons to trade with the "Coal River." Seven years after that, in 1829, I find the item of coal mentioned for the first time amongst the productions of this Colony. In 1829, I think it was, 800 tons of coal, valued at £400, were raised in the district of Newcastle. At that time, also, if I am informed correctly, the only means of communication between Newcastle and Sydney was a single cutter, called the "Lord Liverpool," of eighty tons burden, which frequently occupied two or three weeks on the passage. But how different is the picture which we see around us this day. Why, last year—that is in 1871—790,143 tons of coal were raised from the Northern Coal-fields, of the value of £274,000. Of this 565,000 tons of coal, valued at over a quarter of a million sterling, was exported from the port of Newcastle to twenty-seven Foreign and Inter-colonial ports, in nearly 1,000 vessels. As regards the trade of the port, it appears to me at present to rival that of the metropolitan port of Sydney, as

I find that last year—exclusive altogether of coasters, 1,040 vessels, of 376,000 tons burden, cleared from the Port of Newcastle for Foreign and Intercolonial ports, whilst the total number of vessels clearing from the whole of the Colony, including Newcastle, was only 2,123, whose tonnage was 794,000 tons. In short, Newcastle, which only a few years ago, within the recollection of gentlemen now sitting at this table, was an unimportant, isolated, and almost unknown village on the coast, communicating with Sydney by means of a single cutter of eighty tons burden, is now a large and thriving port, bustling with commercial life and activity, and brought by means of the steamers and the telegraph into intimate association with the outside world. I scarcely remember anything which can compare with the marvellous rapidity with which Newcastle has risen, except some of the incidents which we read of in the fortunes of Aladdin. And I think I may fairly say that your genius of the lamp is your coal. Nor do I think that Newcastle is going to remain stationary. Indeed, looking at what has been done during the last few years, and the vastness of your resources, it is difficult to set bounds to the imagination when contemplating the future of Newcastle, which is destined, I believe, to become one of the greatest of commercial cities in these seas. The place is not only the natural port and outlet for one of the richest and largest agricultural districts in the Colony, with which it is connected by a railway of over 124 miles in length; but, as I have said, it possesses coal deposits of superior quality, capable of being economically worked, conveniently situated for export, and in extent sufficient to supply the world.

KEROSENE.

The Colony is rich in deposits of brown cannel oil coals and oil shales. They exist in many places at wide areas apart, and are so rich that in a very short period the exportation of kerosene shale and oil may be expected to assume great proportions. Preparations are being made for working the valuable seams near Murrurundi, in the Northern district, and for some few years the manufacture of oil has been carried on near Wollongong and at Hartley, from the Hartley shale, which is brought down by railway. The company has invested £100,000 in the manufacture of oil, and their works are very extensive and complete. At the present time they manufacture 8,000 gallons of oil per week, and in about a month hence their manufacturing power will be increased to 12,000 gallons weekly. The price of American kerosene oil, wholesale, in Sydney, is 2s. 7d. per gallon, but the Shale and Oil Company produce an excellent article, which they sell wholesale at 1s. 8d. per gallon, a price which enables them to pay a dividend of 12½ per cent. on their capital. If further proof were needed of the valuable properties of the colonial shale, it may be found in the fact that the company exports large quantities of it for gas-making purposes to Melbourne and San Francisco. Under the present mode of retorting, the shale gives a return of 150 gallons of crude oil to the ton, and after treatment and distillation gives a return of 75 gallons of clear burning oil, besides 25 per cent. of other marketable commodities. A ton of the Hartley coal gives 18,000 feet of gas with an illuminating power equal to forty candles. With a practically unlimited extent of shale land, it is obvious that the manufacture and export of kerosene is likely to go on increasing, and that it will not be long before the manufacturers of this Colony obtain complete possession of the Australian markets.

A visitor to the Company's mine at Hartley, in 1871, gives the following picture of a mining settlement in one of the wildest, most rugged, and, but for the railway, inaccessible parts of Australia :—

Perhaps one of the most pleasing features in this secluded valley is the care which is taken of the social and moral condition of the miners. They have all comfortable residences, and although there is a small store on the ground there is no public-house. A Public School has been established for some time, and the names on the roll number fifty-three, with an average attendance of forty. There are occasional visits from clergymen of the Church of England and the Wesleyan denominations, scarcely a Sunday passing without one or other performing Divine Service in the valley. A medical man is engaged by the Company, and paid a small quarterly sum by the miners. In order to induce a settlement on the ground of a steady fixed population of miners, the Company are about to offer to men in their employ plots of ground sufficient for a house and garden. The freehold of these plots would be sold at a merely nominal price, the Company reserving to themselves the right to all minerals under the surface.

Iron.

Iron ores are widely disseminated throughout the Colony, the principal beds being hematite. Little or nothing, however, has yet been done to bring them into the market, although many inquiries are now being made with a view to commence smelting operations; and it is not unlikely that in the course of the next few years we shall have extensive works at Hartley, near Newcastle, and on the coast of Illawarra, where the richest ores exist side by side with the best bituminous coal and with lime, and in the case of the last named localities there is this further advantage, proximity to water carriage. The attempt to manufacture iron at Nattai on the southern line of railway was commenced some years ago; 4,000 tons were raised in 1865 of the stated value of £1,500. But the coal in the vicinity was not exactly suited to the purpose; and in the absence of the railway, then incomplete, but which now passes through the ground, the carriage of lime and other heavy materials proved fatal to early attempts as a commercial speculation. Want of the requisite skill probably operated as a still greater obstacle. It is expected that the works will soon be re-opened; now that railway carriage is available and the price of iron has advanced. The iron at Nattai is tough, close-grained, easily worked, and contains from sixty-five to seventy per cent. of ore.

In a paper read before the Engineering Association at Sydney, last year, Mr. Croll, a gentleman who has paid considerable attention to the subject, remarked:—

The iron ore which has been wrought has been found to be from 20 to 25 per cent. richer than the iron ore of Great Britain. We have only one ironworks in the Colony; and, I am sorry to say that up to the present time it has been commercially unsuccessful. But although this company has been surrounded by a number of difficulties which are sure to beset a new enterprise in a young colony, they have done sufficient to show that our Colonial iron cannot be surpassed by any iron in the world. They produced iron which was sent home to England, and found to be of superior quality, and suitable for making into a superior kind of steel. About seven years ago I had an opportunity of assisting to test the cohesive strength of our wrought iron in comparison with other iron generally used. The testing was done by getting a number of pieces of the different kinds of iron made with a ring on each end, and a short part in the middle, made in thickness to a quarter of an inch gauge. It was then suspended, and weights were applied until it broke. And it was found that it stood from 50 to 100 lbs. more than different iron used, such as BBH, and several others; and it was only equalled by the Lowmore iron; and if there was any difference the Fitzroy iron was the strongest. At the same time I also saw several experiments tried with the cast-iron bars of about 2 feet long, 1½ x ¾ inch thick. These bars were suspended by each end, and weights applied to the middle until they broke; and by a line being stretched from end to end it was found that it bent over an inch before it broke. This shows the toughness and flexibility of the Colonial cast iron. It is to be regretted that the only iron ore that has been tried has been the Fitzroy ore, although good samples have been found along the coast. A few months ago I was at Orange, and I got a piece of iron ore, the specific gravity of which shows that it is nearly all iron.

Our workers in metals have proved by their industry, ingenuity, and enterprise that they have lost none of the best characteristics of the race from which they have sprung. Our iron beds are almost co-extensive with our coal measures; and, considering the great and special advantages this Colony possesses for trade with Foreign Countries, we may conclude that New South Wales is destined to emulate the industrial greatness of Britain, if not, in the lapse of years, to surpass it. "Every man of thought," says a well known writer on Geology, "must be more or less impressed with the conviction that much of Britain's supremacy in mechanical and manufacturing industry has arisen from the rich and readily accessible coal fields. They are the mainspring of her mechanical power and the stay of her commercial greatness. These two substances, coal and iron, have been the main factors in all recent progress; and that which most broadly distinguishes the Britain of the present from the Britain of preceding centuries is the extended and extending use of these two substances, through the instrumentality of the steam engine." These words will soon be as applicable to New South Wales in the southern hemisphere as they are to Great Britain in the northern belt of the Globe.

COPPER.

Of the copper mines opened to the end of 1871, seven were in the Western District, and two in the South, and the value of their production was £47,275 for that year. During 1872 several other mines have been opened, and are producing a much larger supply. Official statistics are not yet available. The richest copper mines opened are in the vicinity of Bathurst, Orange, and Bourke, in the West, and of Goulburn in the South. In the Orange district outcrops of copper carbonates have been found over an area of twenty miles square. The Monaro and Shoalhaven country is also known to be very rich in copper ores, and companies have within the last few months been formed to work them. Now that the country is being opened by railways and roads, this branch of industry is becoming daily more important and valuable; and, although we are constantly drawing off bodies of miners from South Australia, one of the great wants of the Colony still is skilled miners; and had we but mining engineers of undoubted ability and experience the capitalists of Sydney would at once embark in many mining enterprises from which they are now compelled to stand aloof.

The Rev. W. B. Clarke says: "That copper and tin appear to be as abundant metals here as in Cornwall. Copper has been made known in great abundance within the last year in the far western interior, which was generally considered to be a flat uninteresting desert between the Lachlan, Bogan, and Darling. Coba, about 90 miles S.E. of Fort Bourke, is now a mining district; and having examined them, I can speak favourably of the value of its ores. Some gold has been detected in another quarter nearer the Darling, and iron, which also occurs at Coba, is found on the New Year's Range, S.E. of the junction of the Bogan. Copper is expected also from that Range. The character of that then waste country given by Sir T. L. Mitchell—"low, bare ridges, scanty vegetation, water very scarce, and vast level plains"—will shortly deserve to be exchanged for one of a more valuable kind. Recently copper lodes have been taken up near the head of the Bogan, and I have been impressed with the great value of the whole area between Molong, Croker's Range, and the head of the Bogan River. Similarly we may notice the development of copper to the south of Bathurst, in the Great Cow Flat Mine. In Maneroo, too, there has been found copper alloyed with antimony; and I have a specimen from near Bathurst, in which no less than eighteen ores and other minerals are combined together."

TIN.

The discovery of the tin ores in the Northern Districts of the Colony in 1870 was scarcely less sudden or exciting than that of gold in 1851, although the existence of both of these metals was spoken of by the Rev. W. B. Clarke some years prior to the discovery of their marketable value by the public. The extent of tin-bearing land in the Colony cannot yet be even approximately stated, but the area is known to be very great, and not to be confined to the districts where the miners are now employed. The analogy between tin mining and mining for gold in the early stages is complete, for the process consists simply of washing the tin from the soil through which it is disseminated. The principal centres of this industry in the North are Inverell, Glen Innes, and from Tenterfield right up to the Queensland border, and very important discoveries of this metal have, within the last few weeks, been reported from Albury and other parts of the South-western district. There are six distinct fields in the North. Mr. F. Gregory has reported to the Queensland Government that, having measured 170 miles of creeks and river beds in that part of Queensland which touches the northern boundary of New South Wales, he found on calculating the value on a fair assumption of the average amount of stream tin (irrespective of vein or matrix tin) that it amounts to £13,000,000. No such investigation has been made on behalf of this Colony; but, if Mr. Gregory's data be correct the value of the New South Wales portion of that one field (which is two-thirds of the whole) may be set down at £26,000,000. And our most northerly field is not richer than those which are situated farther south.

The area of land taken up under mineral lease (mostly for tin) in 1872, was 377,515 acres, the deposits upon which amounted to £94,378. Numerous companies were formed in Sydney during the year, but in many instances the tin wealth of the land has been overvalued, so that much loss and disappointment will be the result. The average cost of washing out a ton of tin ore may be set down at £20, and the ore in the Sydney market is now sold at from £60 to £80 per ton according to assay; so that after making every deduction for bags and carriage to market, there is still an ample profit upon any reasonable investment of capital. The latest advices received here by post at the time of writing this pamphlet are contained in Messrs. Mort & Co.'s London circular, dated November 28, 1872. They report:—"The quality of the Australian ingot tin coming forward appears to be remarkably fine. A few tons were sold on the 26th inst. at £136 to £138, while the value of Straits on the same day was only £134. Should this standard be maintained we may look for the Australian production taking a very high rank in the market." London telegrams, dated February 1st, 1873, quote tin at £146 per ton. Tin appeared among the list of exports from New South Wales for the first time last year, and up to the 31st December, the quantity sent away was— ingot tin, 91 tons 18 cwt., stated value, £12,623; and tin ore, 1,031 tons 12 cwt., stated value, £75,955. The total quantity received in Sydney during that year (1872) was 1730 tons 1 cwt., and the stated value, £123,274. Much of this was from the Queensland field, having been sent to Sydney for shipment. Several veins or lodes of tin have been discovered on all the fields in this colony; but work is at present almost exclusively directed to washing the stream or drift tin.

The following remarks on the occurrence of tin in New South Wales, from the pen of the Rev. W. B. Clarke, will probably be read with interest:—

The stream tin must, of course, be quarternary or recent in its present position. Tin stone has been found loose in the bed of the Shoalhaven, but the actual lode has never been discovered. In several other localities tin is known to me as having been found, either as stream tin, or wood tin, in the ordinary gold drifts with other loose minerals—indications, as I consider such instances, of future discoveries in parts of the Colony not yet searched. The great granite masses in this Colony are not, probably, all so richly endowed as some particular spots which are now found so prolific; but, having seen the greater part of them, I am impressed with the opinion that for centuries to come the industry now commenced will continue to occupy a prominent position among the producers of Colonial wealth, just as the mines of Tenasserim, Merghui, and Malacca have not decreased in value since the commencement of their working. In Malacca many of the lodes are horizontal. The average produce of the above-named mines is from 60 to 80 per cent., and its value is reckoned at nearly 4¼ millions per annum.

The only geological examination which has yet been made is that by Mr. Surveyor Wilkinson, who, during the last few months, has been investigating the geological character of the tin-bearing country on Cope's Creek, near Inverell. In a report to the Government, dated 6th December, 1872, he says :—

Hitherto miners have carefully confined their operations to working the recent alluvium in the beds of the creeks; surfacing on the sides of the hills has been carried on to some extent, but the creek drifts have yielded the largest supply of tin ore. Narrow alluvial flats extend along the course of Cope's Creek; in them the alluvium seldom obtains a greater thickness than 20 feet, the wash-dirt scarcely averaging 2 feet thick. In the bed of the creek but little stripping is required, and the wash in places averages 3 feet deep. The yield is from a few ounces up to 8 or 10 pounds weight (in some instances) of stream tin to the dish, and is generally the same in most claims, though some have larger rich patches than others. In Mr. Holme's claim, the "Victoria," between Captain Swinton's station and the Inverell Company's mine, *eleven cwt.* of stream tin in one day have been obtained by twelve men. I have collected statistics from twenty-seven mines, the yield of tin ore up to the present time, together with the number of men employed, &c. These statistics show that 810 were employed for an *average* period of *four months,* and that the total yield of tin ore has been 319 tons; of this, one mine, the "Britannia," has raised 50 tons in six months. In estimating from these data the average earnings per man, it must be remembered that, owing to the inclemency of the weather, floods, and the time required for the erection of necessary improvements and machinery, the miners were not actually employed in raising tin ore probably more than three-quarters of the average time above stated. When the weather becomes more settled, and the miners fully employed, the average returns from Cope's Creek will probably increase. The above-mentioned 319 tons of ore were from only twenty-seven mines. There are other mines in this district which I was unable to visit. However, I believe that the total yield of stream tin from Cope's Creek up to the present time will not much exceed 400 tons. With reference to the richness of the recent alluvial deposits in Cope's Creek, the statistics which I have given above will speak favourably. Some of the smaller claims cannot take long to be worked out, while many others will require several years to exhaust them of their riches, according to the number of men employed and the system of management. I cannot believe that in many cases astonishing rich yields will be revealed, but there can be no doubt that tin mining in this district will become a profitable industry for a numerous population during many years to come. Rich specimens of copper ore found in the district have been shown to me. Sapphires of various colours are of common occurrence with the stream tin in Cope's Creek. Two diamonds are said to have been found in Darby's Branch Creek,—on the Britannia Mine. I am informed that as many as *sixty* diamonds, from one claim, and *forty*, from another, were obtained lately in the Bora or Maid's Creek, a few miles S.W. from the Bundarra, crossing Cope's Creek.

The following paragraphs, clipped from the *Sydney Morning Herald*, December 2, 1872, may serve to give an idea of the value of the tin deposits of the Colony. They are a fair sample of many others which are published in the newspapers daily:—

Mount Mitchell Tin M. Co.—The extract from manager's report of the 28th October: "I forwarded 6 tons 2 cwt. 3 quarters 16 lbs. of tin ore yesterday, and the ground I am working is turning out well. I have been sluicing with only one set of boxes for nine days, for 35 bags tin ore, and expect to extract from 10 to 12 ozs. of gold from the ore. In this ground I expect to realize fully one half of the cost of working in gold alone."

Sydney Tin Company.—Telegram from mining manager, dated 2nd November, states: "Tin ore obtained during the week, over 8 tons, proceeds of six boxes. Sixty men are employed; am sending away 13 tons on 4th November. Have engaged teams for 6 tons more."

Modern Briton Tin.—The manager reports the arrival in Sydney of 476 ingots of tin, weight 6 tons 14 cwt., the produce of this company's mine, and smelted at the Stockton Works, Newcastle.

Ruby Creek Tin Co.—The mining manager reports: "Work delayed this week by the rain. Yield about 3 tons; water supply sufficient. The manager has received, through a mercantile firm of this city, a report from their London brokers on a small parcel of ore sent home per overland mail, the bulk having been shipped by the Narcissus. The brokers give the value, at that date (October 5), of the Ruby Creek ore at £101 10s. per ton in Cornwall, and speak of it as splendid metal."

Rex Tin Co.—The mining manager reports under date of the 5th instant: "We have struck another rich patch. The prospects of the lode are also good. I have consigned to you now 107 bags, and in a few days 50 bags more will follow."

Big Ruby Tin Co.—The mining manager reports: "I have twenty-eight men at work, and the average since starting has been 9 tons per week. I have forwarded 697 bags tin ore, and we have another 6 tons ready to start."

Haslemire Tin M. Co.—The manager reports under date the 6th instant, that the party on the island got 4 bags yesterday afternoon and 8 bags more to-day. He further says: "The seam of ore looks first rate; it is from 12 to 15 inches thick and over 6 feet wide."

Great Dividing Range Tin Co.:—Manager reports: "Expect to send 2 tons a week during dry season, and 10 tons a week as soon as we get full supply of water. In cutting a trench across a large flat we found that the tin was not confined to the creek, but extends across the entire flat. I obtained as much as 10 lbs. to the dish, 170 feet back from the creek, and several pounds to the dish even from some post-holes I sunk. I believe that this flat alone contains over 1,000 tons of tin."

The *Inverell Courier* of the 2nd November, in speaking of the mines at Cope's Creek, remarks :—" Lady Emily : This company are in full work with ten men, and are averaging half a ton per day. Victoria Company commenced sluicing last Wednesday week, and obtained half a ton by Saturday, and 15 cwt. for the week ending last Thursday. This company have suffered severely by the heavy floods. Lyngarr Company have commenced washing, and obtained 13 cwt. for two days' work, with two men and a boy. Parker, Brothers, and Company, have ten men at work, and obtain about 9 cwt. a day with 2 boxes. 7 tons of ore were sent away on Tuesday last. The Rose Company, Flood and party : (First block) Four men are at work, and with 1 box the yield with 3 days' washing was 6 cwt. In the second block, north of the Creek, operations have just been commenced, and 5 cwt. was the result for two days' working, with one box, and they are now engaged stripping two paddocks, in which five men are employed. Alabama Company have four men working, two sets of boxes, the yield being 14 cwt. for the week. Hackett's Downfall have only two men at work, and for one day's washing 2 cwt. was the result. O'Regan and Co.—Morning Star Company—have been prevented by the floods from opening up the ground ; there are six men employed, and the yield of the week has been 1 ton.· The total yield has been 30 tons. Romley and party have two men at work, and they obtain 2½ cwt. per day. Boggy Camp have eleven men employed with two boxes, and raise from half a ton to 12 cwt. per week. They have taken out about 8 tons up to date.

The *Inverell Courier* of the 9th November, speaking of a piece of lode tin recently discovered in the neighbourhood of Cope's Creek, says :—"The specimen, which was a thing to be admired, was in shape something like the half of a small flat cheese, and weighed, we should say, about 20 lbs. It was a mass of tin crystals, encased in a thin layer of dry cement, almost as white as chalk. The sample was taken from a seam or lode of the same consistence, at a depth of 35 feet from the surface, and we were told much finer specimens could be obtained, but that they will not hold together when the cement becomes dry."

In speaking of the recent discoveries, a late issue of the *Albury Banner* says :—" The late finds on the various tributaries of the Upper Murray, on the New South Wales side of the river, bid fair to excel in magnitude and importance the best of the recent discoveries in the neighbourhood of Koetong. The nearest point at which tin in payable quantities is known to exist is

Basin Creek, on the Dorra Dorra run. Commencing from the lower end of the Creek and going upwards, a large block of ground, covering 600 acres, has been leased by Messrs. Fleming, Hayes, and Holman. Higher up, on the same creek, a still larger block has been taken up, 800 acres having been leased by Messrs. Hayes, Brothers, Holman, and Williams. In almost all parts of the claim a prospect of a quarter of a pound of tin to the dish. The ground appears also to be peculiarly adapted for the carrying on of sluicing operations. At the end of the claim there is an abrupt descent of fully 20 feet, so that by cutting through a very small portion of rock a tail race with a capital fall could be easily excavated. A sample of the tin ore from this vicinity, on being assayed, gave a return of seventy-two per cent. of pure metal. Still proceeding up the river, the next tin country of any importance is the Jinjellic Swamp, and here four tin lodes have been discovered. The first prospectors were Day and Co., who have applied for an 80-acre lease. During the past week the remaining three lodes were struck by Messrs. Williams and Holman, who have also applied for 80 acres adjoining, and parallel with, the claim of Messrs Day and Co. A large number of claims have been taken up by Messrs. Wellington, Swift, and others, for streaming purposes; these latter claims being of course on the lower ground. It is believed that the lodes will run down to the creek, as the tin washed is of a course heavy description. On Lanky's Creek the whole ground is taken up, and several parties are engaged in cutting tail races, in order to commence work in a systematic manner. The whole of the ground on the main Jinjellic Creek has also been leased, and will, no doubt, in a short time be in thorough working order. At the Horse Creek the tin lodes were first discovered by Holman and Williams, who have, in conjunction with Messrs. Hayes, Brothers, secured four 25-acre blocks. No less than four well-defined lodes run through this property, and pieces of pure ruby tin, from 1 to 10 ozs. in weight, are frequently met with. Tin has already been traced from Jinjellic to the Ten-mile Creek, and every day brings news of some fresh discovery."

SILVER, LEAD, CINNABAR, DIAMONDS, &C.

There are silver and lead mines near Yass, in the Southern Districts (the ore from which has been sent to England to be separated), and near Scone, on the Hunter. There are also deposits of silver ore at Broulee, near Moruya. Cinnabar is found in the Mudgee district, and antimony ores have been worked in the Clarence district.

Some twenty years ago (says the *Bathurst Free Press* of February, 1873), Dr. Machattie purchased a portion of land in the neighbourhood of Brownlea, under the impression that a payable silver mine would be discovered thereon. A shaft was sunk on the land, and some prospecting ensued, with very promising results; but from some cause or other the work was not proceeded with. Since that time the land has become the property of Mr. J. M'Phillamy, and recently, operations on the mine have again been commenced. A shaft has been sunk, and at the depth of about 68 feet the lode was cut. A portion of the ore was raised and sent to Mr. Cawse, of the Icely Mines, for assay. A statement of the result of the assay has been received, and the report is considered very satisfactory, the yield of silver being at the rate of nearly 48 ozs. to the ton of ore.

The number of diamonds found in New South Wales up to the 31st December, 1872, was estimated at between 5,000 and 6,000, the largest having been one of 5¼ carats, and the smallest one-tenth of a grain. The average weight is about one grain. Opals, rubies, topaz, and other gems have been found in many parts of the Colony. The *Sydney Morning Herald*, February, 1873, reports :—

In the beginning of this year, also, there have been exhibited at the Bank of New South Wales, Sydney, a package of 375 diamonds, recently found at the Bingera diggings. Of the character of the stones there can be no doubt; they are one and all true diamonds, but their commercial value is trifling. With one exception, they are of small size, the bulk "off coloured," and many of them little better than "cleavage." Amongst them are a few octahedrons of good water. The largest stone is of irregular shape, fractured at one end, and flawed internally. They certainly prove that diamonds exist in the northern districts; and where those were found, larger and finer stones may yet turn up.

Queensland has not long retained the honor of being the only opal-producing Colony in Australia. We have not to go away from home to find a mine of that description. Any person who is dubious upon the point should pay a visit to Mr. Jones, jeweller, George-street, where there are now on exhibition a number of cut and uncut opals, and about twenty pieces of clay-porphyry, sparkling with these gems in the matrix. Amongst the polished stones are some of the harlequin class. These are of a lighter colour than the Queensland stones previously exhibited at the same establishment, which had the peculiar tinge which scientists attribute to the presence of oxide of iron, and is the rarest variety. The New South Wales mine is situated at Rocky Bridge Creek, New Abercrombie River, and is the property of Messrs. Emanuel and Magonnis.

Mineral Lands: How obtained.

Under the Crown Lands Occupation Act, leases are granted to all who apply for them of land not exceeding 320 acres, nor less than 40 acres, for coal mining lots, and not exceeding 80 nor less than 20 acres for other mineral lots, for the purpose of mining for any mineral excepting gold, at a yearly rental of 5s. per acre, the leases not to exceed fourteen years, but to be renewable at the end of that time for fourteen years more. Lessees have to spend at the rate of £5 an acre during the first three years of their leases. They can throw up their leases at any time by giving three months' notice to the Minister for Lands; or can convert them into mineral purchases on payment of £2 per acre, and making improvements to the value of £5 per acre.

Mineral leases, other than gold, issued up to the 31st December, 1872, were, for coal, 34,720 acres; other minerals (principally tin and copper), 396,228 acres. Total, 430,948 acres.

VI.—MANUFACTURING INDUSTRIES.

The great mass of the working population has hitherto been employed in the production of raw materials rather than in their manufacture. Within the last few years, however, great advances have been made in mechanical development; costly plants of all the most approved labour-saving appliances and steam-driven tools have been introduced, so that the mechanics of the Colony are now able to compete successfully with those of Europe in the supply of local requirements. They earn much higher wages than are paid in Europe; but as a set-off against this, the local manufacturer has the benefit of the greater cheapness of the raw material, the advantage afforded by freight of imported manufactured articles, and of his own knowledge of local requirements and ability to speedily supply them. Workmen and tools were in the first instance needed to effect repairs; and the skill required for that purpose, being equal to the work of construction, has gradually extended its operations, until now many flourishing factories have been established as the natural result of our circumstances, and without the fostering care of the State. The policy of the Parliament has uniformly been what is known as free-trade. The Colony at present offers little scope for those industries which require a minute subdivision of skilled labour, and which depend for their existence on a practically unlimited market; but at the same time there is ample scope here for many new industries, and it may well be doubted whether any other Colony offers a more promising field in this direction.

Iron Trades.

In the foremost rank of artizans must be placed the workers in metal, who number more than four thousand. The largest engineering establishments in Australia are situated in Sydney.

One of them employs 750 hands, and two others each gives constant employment to between 300 and 400 hands. The works of the Australasian Steam Navigation Company are chiefly employed in repairing and enlarging their splendid fleet of ocean steamships, and the engineering establishment of Messrs. Mort and Co. is also largely engaged in marine work of that description. This establishment built an iron steamship of 500 tons for the Queensland Government, a year or two ago; and we now have the men and machinery in the port to construct steamships three times that size. Messrs. P. N. Russell and Co. have built large and powerful dredges for the Colonial Governments, a turret-ship for New Zealand, and other works implying the existence of high mechanical skill with large and varied resources. They have also a very extensive factory for making railway rolling stock. Several locomotives of great power have been built in the Colony, and are now running upon our railways. Messrs. Vale and Lacey and Messrs. Mort and Co. are engaged upon the construction of eighteen locomotive engines for the Colonial Government, in addition to those they have already made. The first and most powerful locomotive, for goods and passenger traffic, was made under the direction of the Engineer-in-Chief for the Government Railways, at the Redfern workshops. It was completed in June, 1870, and has been running on the Southern line ever since. The total weight of the engine under steam is 33 tons 14 cwt., and of the tender 22 tons 10 cwt. The iron lighthouses on the Southern coast, which are more than fifty feet high, and remarkable for elegance, symmetry, and strength, were made under the direction of the Engineer-in-Chief for Harbours and Rivers, at Mr. Mather's establishment, in Sydney; and there are several engineering firms both here and at Newcastle which are capable of executing very large works. Having regard to the extent of our mercantile marine, it must be obvious that there is constant work for a very large number of engineers and machinists upon repairing work alone, and when to this is added the large demand which has sprung up for iron work in connection with flour-mills, sugar-mills, quartz-crushing-mills, sheep washing and stone breaking apparatus, bridges (iron road and railway bridges, with the most massive cylindrical piers, having been constructed, varying in length from 150 to 500 feet), and machinery of all descriptions—it is clear that this branch of industry, for which the Colony possesses special facilities, is destined to assume vast proportions. Steam hammers, turning, boring, punching, cutting, bending, and riveting machines exist in all the large establishments. We have appliances for turning and boring up to 14 feet, and for planing up to 25 feet 6 inches. Iron castings can be made in one piece up to 30 tons, and brass castings up to 10 tons.

There are two graving docks in the port of Sydney, capable of taking in the largest ships which trade in the Pacific, and which can at any time be enlarged if the requirements of the port rendered that necessary; and the Government propose to construct a third, which is to be of still greater dimensions.

We have also two galvanized iron factories, which make up all the tubs, buckets, and articles of that description required in the Colony.

Smelting Works.

Smelting works for the reduction of tin and copper ores are now becoming an important branch of industry; and it is even found profitable to send the poorest copper ores from South Australia to be smelted at Newcastle. The smelting works are chiefly in the neighbourhood of our Coal Fields, and the following facts, respecting the Governor's visit to one of them (Hunter River Company's, at Waratah), will show the character and magnitude of the operations carried on at several of these establishments:—

The works comprise twenty-one furnaces, seventeen of which were in full work, so that nearly all the processes of copper-smelting and refining were witnessed. His Excellency was shown the mode of reducing the ore, the roasting of the regulus, and the tapping of the regulus and coarse copper. Several furnaces were tapped or raked out in the presence of the whole party. About 20,000 tons of what is termed third-class ore is smelted at these works every year. The stuff is brought up from Wallaroo, South Australia. The vessels engaged in transporting the ore take cargoes of coal from Newcastle to South Australia, for the purpose of smelting the best of the ore at the mines, and on their return journey they bring up the poor ore, which it would be too expensive to smelt with imported coal at Wallaroo. Four new furnaces have been lately erected, and will soon be at work. The quantity of ore operated upon will then, it is expected, amount to about 25,000 or 30,000 tons every year. There are now about 120 men engaged at the works. The production of pure copper averages about 1,800 or 2,000 tons a year, and the consumption of coal in the furnaces about 26,000 tons.

F

Ship and House-building.

Ship-building and other industries to which timber is indispensable may be said to be specially and magnificently endowed by Nature in New South Wales, for the forests along her Pacific coast supply timbers of the most valuable and varied character, and would, but for the ruthless destruction which goes on in new lands taken up by settlers, whether in Australia or America, last for ages. Some years ago we imported many thousand pounds worth of timber yearly; but now we scarcely import anything, and as may be seen from Statistics in the Appendix, our forests furnish a large and valuable export trade. Licenses to cut timber (£1 a year for hardwood, and £3 for cedar) are granted to all who apply for them, so that the Government practically makes a gift of its forests to the timber-using industries of the Colony. Large reserves have, however, recently been made. There are several steam saw-mills in various parts of the Colony, some of them employing from 59 to 100 hands.

The hardwood timbers of the Colony are well adapted for ship, house, and carriage building, and many other purposes. Some descriptions of it, placed in wells and buried in the ground, have been taken up after the lapse of fifty years and upwards, and found to be as sound as on the day they were immured or immersed. Our best timbers are near water carriage, and the rivers along the coast all offer superior facilities for shipbuilding, timber as sound and durable as any yet known being there ready to hand. Of the ten thousand forest trees which probably represent the timber-producing capabilities of the globe, seven or eight thousand would flourish in New South Wales.

The largest ship-building establishment in Sydney is that of Mr. John Cuthbert, who employs two hundred hands. The total number of men employed on wood is 6,300. The aggregate tonnage of vessels built in the Colony is 76,700 tons. Ironbark is well suited for keels, kelsons, stringers, and, in fact, any part of a ship requiring strength. For length, straightness of growth, and lasting quality it is probably without an equal. The gum is well adapted for planking, and the blackbut makes first-class treenails, while the non-shrinking qualities of the beech have marked it out for decks and other fittings. Timber for crooks can be obtained in any quantity, and of the best quality. For a few pounds the shipbuilder can cut and cart away as much timber as will last him the whole of the year, and it is estimated that the proprietors of saw-mills take 100,000 feet of timber for every £1 they pay to Government for license to cut. Shipbuilding is carried on on the Richmond, Clarence, Manning, and the Clyde Rivers, at Brisbane Water, Terrigal, Cape Hawke, and Jervis' Bay. Twenty years ago the average size of vessels built was from 15 to 50 tons, but the average now runs from 50 to 500 tons. Many fine faithfully-built vessels of about 300 tons have been completed in the ship-building yards along the coast, but ship-building for export sale has not yet been carried on to any great extent. Mr. Cuthbert is building four fine schooners, models of symmetry, for the Admiralty, intended for service in the South Sea Islands. Naval officers of the Imperial Government have spoken in terms of the highest praise of the two which have already been launched. The timber in Colonial vessels is found to be perfectly sound after the lapse of thirty and forty years.

All the wood-work used in house-building is fashioned with steam-driven tools, and for the requirements of the joiner the cedar and pine are admirably adapted. The former especially takes an excellent polish, and is richer and more handsome in appearance than mahogany; it is very durable, and it has the great recommendation of being easily worked. It is largely used for skirting-boards, window-sashes, doors, furniture, and the interior fittings of houses. The proprietor of a steam saw-mill and joinery factory, who employs eighty hands, writes, under date January 17th, 1872: "I wish we could get more men at these rates [see Chapter XIV]. There are more demands on us for work now than we can execute."

Coach and Carriage Trades.

The coach and carriage trade has grown rapidly during the last few years; and the best tribute to the skill of our workmen in this department of industry is to be found in the thousands of well appointed equipages, which daily run along the thoroughfares of the capital. For buggy-work, which requires the combination of strength and lightness, American hicory has to be imported. For all other purposes, our own timbers are better adapted than anything we can buy. All the cabs, carriages, carts, drays, omnibuses, and other vehicles required are made in the Colony.

Stone and Earth.

The Colony is well off as regards building materials of all kinds. Freestone may be hewn out of the quarries around Sydney of any size. The key-stone of one of the arches in the new General Post Office, laid by H.R.H. the Duke of Edinburgh, weighed nearly 30 tons. In the same building there are nearly 50 highly polished columns of grey granite, from the Moruya quarries. The supply of every description of stone requisite for building houses, docks, &c., is unlimited and easily accessible. Marble quarries, limestone, and all sorts of clay, excepting kaolin, are found; and the manufacture of bricks, encaustic tiles, drain-pipes, and other descriptions of pottery is carried on by the aid of steam-driven machinery. The workers in stone and earth number 3,600.

Leather, &c.

The manufacture and working-up of leather gives employment to 5,200 men. Some of the boot and shoe factories of Sydney employ between three and four hundred hands, who are engaged chiefly in the manufacture of strong boots, for which there is a great demand in the Colony, and for export to New Zealand and Queensland. Women's and children's boots, and a good deal of light harness, are still imported. Our manufacturers of leather, boots, &c., have provided themselves with the best machinery from England; and until the Customs duty was increased from ten to twenty per cent. *ad valorem*, in Victoria, they were exporting largely to that Colony. The export of hides, leather, boots, and shoes, the produce of the Colony, in 1871, was of the value of £177,262. 80,652 cwt. of soap, and 13,568 cwt. of tallow candles, were made in the Colony in 1871. Kerosene oil and stearine candles are, however, chiefly used.

Woollen Cloths.

The Colony possesses a special advantage for the production of fine wool; and for some years past woollen cloths of a rough description have been made here. The more attractive patterns and finish of English textures, however, give them almost complete command of the market. But the produce of Colonial looms has greatly improved within the last few years by the importation of better machinery. Colonial tweeds being made of wool without any admixture of shoddy, are more durable than those we import, and are intrinsically superior. In 1871 we had seven factories, which produced 267,196 yards of cloth and tweeds.

MANUFACTURES, &C., IN NEW SOUTH WALES.

An attentive perusal of the subjoined list of manufactures, works, &c., in New South Wales in 1871, taken from the Official Statistics, will give a fair view of existing manufacturing appliance, and will help to shew the workman what are his chances of obtaining employment in the Colony, and the capitalist what openings exist for new industries :—

Connected with, or dependent upon Agriculture :—Agricultural Implement, 22 ; Tobacco, 33 ; Bakeries (steam), 6 ; Reaping and Thrashing Machines, 657 ; Hay-cutting Machines (steam), 1 ; Hay-pressing Machines, 190 ; Chaff-cutters, 915 ; Bone-manure, 10 ; Wine-presses, 243 ; Sugar, 57 ; Mowing Machines, 211 ; Corn-crushers, 257 ; Corn-shellers, 1,871 ; Maizena and Starch, 1 , Harrows (steam), 1 ; Ploughs (steam), 1 ; Winnowing Machines; 604.

Working on raw materials, the production of the Pastoral interest :—Soap and Candles, 31 ; Woollen Cloths, 7 ; Tanneries, &c., 130 ; Fellmongers, &c., 31 ; Salting and Meat-preserving Establishments, 19 ; Boiling-down Establishments, 44 ; Wool-washing establishments, 35 ; Wool-washing Machines (steam), 2 ; Wool-pressing Machines (steam), 27 ; Glue Manufactory, 1 ; Sheep-washing Machines, 43.

Manufacture of Food, of which the raw material is not the produce of Agriculture, and of articles of drink :—Distilleries and Sugar Refineries, 57 ; Breweries, 24 ; Confectionery Manufactories, 26 ; Coffee, Chocolate, and Spice Works, 6 ; Ginger-beer, Liqueurs, Ærated Waters, Cordial, Vinegar, Ink, and Blacking Manufactories, 92 ; Jam Manufactories, 1 ; Building Materials and Plastic Manufactories, Brick-yards, 257 ; Drain-pipe, 1 ; Lime-kilns, 121 ; Potteries, &c., 12 ; Tile-works, 4 ; Saw-mills, &c., 112.

Machine Manufactories, Brass, Lead, and Iron Works :—Iron and Tin Works, 36 ; Iron, Brass, and Copper Foundries, 31 ; Machinists, Engineers, &c., 79 ; Type Foundries, 2.

Miscellaneous Works and Manufactories:—Air-engine, for working Machinery, 1; Account-books, &c., 7; Bark-cutting Machines, 54; Bark-pressing Machines, 7; Bone-charcoal Manufactory, 1; Boot Manufactories, 37; Brush Manufactories, 1; Cabinet Works (steam), 1; Chemical Works, 2; Clothing Manufactories, 11; Coach and Waggon Manufactories, 89; Dry Docks and Floating Docks, 3; Dye, 9; Firework Manufactory, 1; Fire Engines, 24; Gas Works, 6; Glass, 1; Hat, 9; Ice, 3; Kerosene Oil, 2; Mast and Block Manufactories, 3; Organ Builders, 1; Packing-case Manufactories, 4; Paper Mills, 2; Patent Slips, 5; Printing Establishments (steam), 9; Rope, 4; Railway Carriage Works, 3; Salt Works, 2; Ship and Boat Builders, 86; Shirt Manufactories, 4; Smelting Works—Iron, Copper, and Tin, 10; Soap Powder Manufactory, 1; Steam Joinery, 1; Steam-vessels, 98; Steam-washing Machines, 3; Stone-crushing Machines, 6; Stone-dressing Machine, 1; Waterworks, 4. Total, 6,827.

Gold Mining Machinery:—Steam-engines employed in winding, pumping, &c., No. 101, aggregate horse power, 1193. (In alluvial mining) puddling machines, 245; whims and pulleys, 248; whips, 271; sluices and toms, 415; water-wheels, 98; hydraulic hoses, 22; pumps, 237; sluice-boxes, 1,098; derricks, 15; stamp-heads, 50; boring-machines, 2. (In quartz mining) crushing-machines, 76; stamp heads, 735; whims and pulleys, 78; water-wheels, 15; derricks, 34; whips, 37; concave buddles, 2.

VII.—REVENUE: BANKS, &c.

The Revenue of New South Wales, during last year, was £4,775,540, and the expenditure £3,722,922, leaving a credit balance on the year of £1,052,618. This is inclusive of loan and trust funds. The revenue proper of the year was £2,812,379, and the expenditure upon the public service, £1,745,039; so that the surplus of income over outgoings was £1,067,340, and if to this be added loans paid off, the year's surplus would stand at

£1,460,171. The following statement shows the principal heads of revenue for the last two years:—

	The year 1871.	The year 1872.		In the year.
Customs	£860,116	£974,857	increase	£114,741
Excise	209,475	221,422	,,	11,947
Stamps	77,500	94,298	,,	16,798
Post Office	84,028	96,477	,,	12,449
Telegraphs	31,769	48,866	,,	17,097
Railways	361,426	421,888	,,	60,462
Crown Lands	497,960	840,452	,,	342,492
Gold	26,924	35,196	,,	8,272
The Mint	18,888	17,789	decrease	1,099
Miscellaneous	70,814	61,134	,,	9,680
Totals	£2,238,900	£2,812,379	Net increase	£573,479

After all, the revenue of a State is one of the best tests of the prosperity of a people, and anyone who will consider the significance of the figures here set down, will see that the wealth of New South Wales is very generally distributed, a fact which is exemplified in the spending power of the people. The taxation proper amounts to £2 10s. 1¼d. per head of the population, that is, basing the calculation on the estimated population of the Colony on the 30th June, 1872, which according to the Registrar General's returns was 527,682. As a matter of fact, the pressure of taxation is light compared with the ability to pay, and being almost wholly derived through the Customs, it is really not felt at all. The machinery of Government has now been established all over the Colony, so that every good citizen who is added to the population, not only contributes to the wealth and happiness of the community, but diminishes the cost of Government.

The total amount of gold coined at the Sydney Mint since it was opened 14th May, 1855, to 31st December, 1872, was £32,354,000.

The sworn returns of the nine Banks in Sydney, published by the Government, shew that on the 31st December, 1872 (the latest date available), they held deposits to the amount of £9,273,086, and that their total assets were £13,923,791. The total paid-up capital was £7,674,656. The rates per annum of last dividend were 6, 7, 8, 8, 8, 12, 12½, 13, and 20 per cent.; the total amount of the year's divided profits being £409,247. If to these monetary institutions, established for facilitating the operations of commerce, were added the savings of the humbler classes deposited in the New South Wales Savings' Bank and the Post Office Savings' Banks, the amount of deposits would be vastly increased. The total amount at the credit of depositors in the Savings' Bank of New South Wales on the same date was £1,028,737 ; and if to this be added the reserved and other funds, the total was £1,176,850. The total deposits in the Money Order Offices on the 31st December, 1872, was £109,343. The Colony offers great facilities for the investment of capital, not simply in direct mining and industrial enterprises, but also in the stock of the various banking, steam navigation, coal, insurance (fire, life, and marine), gas, and other companies, the rates of last year's dividends varying from 5 to 20 per cent. on the capital invested.

The Auditor General of the Colony has instituted the following comparisons of the progress of accumulation in the paper from which we have already quoted :—

The coin and bullion in the Sydney branch of the Royal Mint, in the Colonial Treasury, and in the Banks of the Colony, on the 31st December, 1871, amounted to £2,522,387, being an increase of 74 per cent. on the amount on the same day of the previous year. A comparison between the first and second five years of the decade shows an average of £1,278,151 for the first period, £1,904,855 for the second; *i.e.*, an increase of nearly 50 per cent.

But it is to the amount on deposit in the several Banking Institutions that we must look for evidence for the accumulated wealth of the people. I find then, that at the end of 1871 the sworn returns of the Banks showed that they held on deposit no less than £7,043,885

N. S. W. Savings' Banks 931,688
Post Office ditto 14,226

Together £7,989,799

This was at the rate of £15 17s. 1d. per head of the population. And it seems to have been in excess of the deposits at the end of the previous year by nearly a million sterling. Dividing the decennary into two equal parts, it will be found that the average annual deposits in the Banks during the earlier five years were £5,713,974, and in the latter five years £6,490,091, showing an increase of between 13 and 14 per cent.

VIII.—TRADE.

There were 4,014 vessels engaged in the trade of the Colony during 1871, whose aggregate tonnage was 1,490,479 (*i.e.* including vessels inward and outward bound). About two-thirds of the whole of the Australian shipping is owned by New South Wales, namely 75,224 tons.

During 1871 the import trade of the Colony was at the rate of £19 1s. 3d., and the export trade at the rate of £22 6s. 2d. per head of the population, that is more than double the import trade and nearly treble the export trade of Great Britain per head of the population for the same year. We may thus classify it:—

UNITED KINGDOM.

Imports from	£3,252,617	
Exports to	4,378,281	
		£7,630,898

AUSTRALIAN COLONIES AND NEW ZEALAND.

Imports from	£5,528,104	
Exports to	6,508,802	
		£12,036,906

FOREIGN COUNTRIES.

Imports from	£828,787	
Exports to	357,949	
		£1,186,736

Total trade 1871...........................£20,854,540

The following statement shows the extent to which New South Wales is now contributing to the wealth of the world by the exportation of her own products:—

	1871.	1872.
Wool	£4,748,160	£2,496,509
Tallow	245,727	213,150
Gold*	2,074,937	2,387,251
Coal	256,690	307,861
Grain (Maize, &c.)	126,957	141,337
Butter and Cheese	40,003	27,619
Live stock	41,330	48,726
Salted and Preserved Meats	133,266	150,762
Hides, Leather, Boots and Shoes	117,262	264,534
Timber	28,455	38,038
Copper*	239,446	376,233
Tin*	......	89,578
Kerosene Oil	11,820	7,679
„ Shale	4,466	7,248
Lead Ore	5,919	231
Antimony Ore	560	5

* Inclusive of what is sent to Sydney and Newcastle for coinage and smelting.

The foregoing list only comprises the principal commodities; and the amounts put down for wool, tallow, live stock, &c., for 1872, do not include the large export trade overland to Victoria.

To the end of 1871, New South Wales exported 733,248,693 lbs. wool, of the value of £50,388,813 ; tallow, 2,136,175 cwts., of the value of £3,365,589'; oil to the value of £2,801,660 ; gold, £40,095,823 ; coal, £3,790,223 ; and large quantities of leather, hides, timber, minerals, fruits, and other native productions.

The position of New South Wales is most favourable for commerce; and Sydney will inevitably become the great emporium for the trade of the Pacific; for nowhere else can there be found a more magnificent haven for ships, and that backed up by a Country the productions of whose soil and whose mineral wealth are more varied, rich, and extensive than most others.

A fair idea of the progressive development of the trade of the Colony during the last ten years, may be gained from a consideration of the following observations, made before the Royal Society by Mr. Christopher Rolleston, the Auditor General of the Colony, in December, 1872. He says:—

I have looked through the statistics of the Board of Trade for the last ten years, and I cannot find amongst all the dependencies of the British Crown—British India excepted—any trade that approaches in value to that of "Australia."

The Colonies are not separately specified in the returns, but as it may be interesting to show what rank the Australian Colonies take amongst "the British Possessions" in their trade with the Mother country, I will take leave to quote the following figures from the Statistical Abstract for 1871.

Imports into Great Britain in the year 1870 from—

British India	£25,090,163
Australia	14,075,264
North American Colonies	8,515,364
West India Islands and Guiana	5,949,199
Ceylon	3,450,974
Cape of Good Hope	2,873,910
The Straits Settlements	2,547,320
All other Possessions	2,330,219
Total	£64,832,413

Exports from Great Britain in 1870 to—

British India	£20,093,749
Australia	10,735,481
North American Colonies	7,584,427
West India Islands and Guiana	3,639,011
Hongkong	3,570,733
The Straits Settlements	2,407,577
Cape of Good Hope	1,962,377
Malta	1,156,982
All other Possessions	4,240,995
Total	£55,391,332

The imports from Australia were 22 per cent. of the whole, and the exports to Australia were 19 per cent. of the whole.

But to return to our own statistics, it should be notified that our trade with Great Britain constitutes no preponderating share of the whole, for I find that in the ten years we imported from Great Britain to the value of £32,575,549; Australian and other Colonies, £37,926,609; foreign countries, £14,330,145; that is to say, from Great Britain, 40 per cent.; other colonies, 42 per cent.; foreign countries, 17 per cent.; as also in exports during the same period, we exported to Great Britain to the value of £30,208,485; Australian and other colonies, £41,467,718; and foreign countries, £2,472,673, that is to say at the rate of 41 per cent., 56 per cent., and 3 per cent. respectively.

It may be interesting here to notice the extent to which the export trade is indebted to the produce and manufactures of the country, because the prosperity of the Colony may be judged by the productions over and above its own wants of articles, the result of its own people's industry. Well, in this point of view, we may derive satisfaction from the returns; for I find that of the exports valued at £74,148,876, for the ten years, no less than £52,043,742 represent the produce and manufactures of New South Wales, exhibiting an annual average of over five millions sterling, and at the rate of £12 3s. 6d. per head of the population.

It has already been shown that the exports of Great Britain for the same period were at the rate of £5 16s. per head of the population. Relatively, therefore, the wealth of this community has been increasing in a ratio more than double that of the Mother Country; there may, perhaps, be two reasons assigned for this: The one refers to the great natural resources of the country which yield their riches with comparatively small assistance from man. The other refers to what I conceive to be the more effective condition of our population. If the productive class bears a larger proportion to the unproductive in one country than in another, the power of creating wealth will be by so much increased. I have reason to believe that when the "Census" of Great Britain in 1871 is compared with that of New South Wales, it will be found that the population, ineffective by reason of age, bears a higher ratio to the aggregate numbers in Great Britain than it does in New South Wales.

The wealth-producing power of population is fully exemplified; for we see that, excepting the one period marked by the dismemberment of Port Phillip, as the population increased so did the power of production, and in an increased ratio.

The import and export trade per head of the population was as follows, viz.:—

In 1831	£15	18	4	per head
1841	25	4	2	,,
1851	17	0	10	,,
1861	33	9	1	,,
And in 1871	40	3	4	,,

We appear to be on the threshold of an epoch of excitement and prosperity; and whoever may live to see the decade out may have a marvellous story to tell of the country's progress, far outstripping that which I have been able to show you to-night.

IX.—HARBOURS AND RIVERS.

There are several commodious harbours along our coast, and in this particular New South Wales has been more highly favoured than any of the Colonies on the Australian Continent. The coast-line is well lighted from north to south, and large sums of money are spent yearly in improving the navigation of the principal harbours and rivers. Storm signals are placed on all the principal promontories, which, together with the seaports, are connected by means of the electric wire with Sydney.

The Richmond River would be navigable for vessels of largest draught for distances of 90 and 50 miles along the two arms into which this noble stream divides; but the trade is now confined to ships of light draught by reason of the sandbar at the entrance. This is one of the richest but most recently settled districts of the Colony, and population there is not yet numerous enough to justify the Government in constructing a breakwater.

The Clarence River is navigated daily by oceam steam-ships for a distance of 50 miles to Grafton, which is becoming the emporium of the north-western trade of the Colony. The width of the stream is nowhere less than half-a-mile. 10,000 persons are settled along its banks, which are clothed with most luxuriant growths of sugar-cane, maize, arrowroot, bananas, vines, and semi-tropical vegetation.

The Bellinger, the Nambuckra, the Macleay, the Hastings, and the Manning Rivers occur farther South. Their productions are similar to those of the Clarence and Richmond; and they have steam communication with Sydney once a week and oftener. Trial Bay, half-way between Sydney and Queensland, is an excellent shelter for all classes of ships during S. and S.E. gales.

The water area of Port Stephens, 25 miles north of Newcastle, is even greater than that of Port Jackson, but there are several sandbanks in it. It runs into the country due west for about 14 miles.

Newcastle is at the mouth of the Hunter River, which is daily navigated by ocean steamships as far as Morpeth, a distance of 29 miles. There is a magnificent breakwater at Newcastle, and many thousand pounds have been expended by the Government in the improvement of this fine seaport.

Broken Bay, at the mouth of the Hawkesbury, is a very capacious harbour, 16 miles north of Sydney Heads, and inferior only to that of Sydney in the draught of water at the entrance, which is limited to 12 feet.

Eight miles to the south of Sydney is Botany Bay, where Captain Cook first landed in Australia. It receives the waters of Cook's and George's Rivers, and has an area of twenty square miles.

Wollongong, Kiama, Shoalhaven (on the river of that name), Ulladulla, and Moruya are small harbours on the south-east coast, where breakwaters, wharfs, and jetties, adapted to the coasting trade, have been constructed.

Twofold Bay is the most southerly port of the Colony. It is five miles deep, east and west, and three miles broad.

Jervis Bay and other places along the south-eastern coast are resorted to as harbours of refuge.

There is regular weekly, bi-weekly, and daily communication by steam-ships between Sydney and the south-eastern coast settlements.

The inland rivers flowing westward are navigated by small steamers from Adelaide in South Australia, which at certain periods of the year go up as far as Wagga Wagga on the Murrumbidgee in the south-west, and Bourke on the Darling in the north-west of the Colony.

X.—FISHERIES.

The rivers and coast of New South Wales abound with fish, and the rocky ledges of all its bays and estuaries form natural oyster beds thousands of miles in length. Sydney and the chief towns of the Colony are plentifully supplied with shell and other fish at all seasons of the year. Some attention is now being paid to the protection and development of our oyster fisheries, and they may ultimately become a large industry. At present our exports are confined to the neighbouring Colonies.

There is a splendid opening for deep sea fisheries, for in that direction nothing is attempted beyond the supply of the local market. "New South Wales," says Mr. A. Oliver, "presents to the eye a coast-line of some 600 miles in length, situated in a zone of temperature, and endowed with marine and topographical conditions admirably adapted as a habitat for the many families of edible fishes with which Nature has endowed us. From north to south the coast abounds both with spawning as well as feeding grounds. A score of rivers, with wide and well protected embouchures, and a thousand inlets and indentations of every size and form, from the vast expanse of Jervis or Broken Bay to the miniature boat-harbour of Terrigal, or the spacious crescent of Curranulla, or Providence Bight, offer all the requirements of sea-bottom for food and protection for the young fry necessary to our southern fish in their various stages of growth."

In 1871 we had five ships employed in the whale fisheries of the Pacific, the total value of whose cargoes is set down at £11,749. In the early days of the Colony the value of our exports of oil in some years amounted to nearly a quarter of a million sterling, as, for instance, in 1841, when it was set down at £224,000. From 1857, however, this trade has been altogether lost to us. Two years ago the Legislature was induced to remit all port charges upon whaling vessels, and to take off the duty upon all articles required by vessels engaged in that trade. So soon as the fact shall have become generally known, we may expect that the whaling fleets of the Pacific will again make Sydney the port at which they will refit and dispose of their cargoes. The reappearance of whale oil among the list of our exports is probably the first-fruits of a revival of that trade.

XI.—THE PORT AND CITY OF SYDNEY.

The following brief description of the Port and City of Sydney in 1869 is taken from a work on the "Industrial Progress of N. S. Wales":—Sydney—once the capital of the Australian Continent, and of New South Wales, when it included Victoria and Queensland—remains the metropolis of New South Wales. Gifted by Nature with all the physical requirements of a great city, the emporium of a Country profusely endowed with mineral wealth, and rich in pastoral and agricultural resources—our city, the "Queen of the Pacific," has increased in importance so largely that at the present time she is entitled to take rank among the principal cities of the World. Within easy sail of, and in constant steam communication with, the neighbouring Colonies, Sydney enjoys a regular intercourse with California, the French settlement of New Caledonia, the Fiji Islands, now rising into commercial importance; she has a trade with many other islands of the Polynesian Group, with the numerous islands of Malaysia, as well as with Southern India. Her ships, also, have an established traffic with China and Mauritius; her immense trade in coal extends far north and westward to the American shores of the Pacific; and her European mail service is carried on by lines of steamers that jointly make a circuit of the earth. Her maritime enterprise is aided by the vast advantages of a noble harbour, on the southern shore of which Sydney is built. Port Jackson, if equalled, is certainly not surpassed by any other natural harbour in the World, and not even by the magnificent haven of Rio Janeiro. The bold coast fronting the Pacific is suddenly broken, and the giant cliffs form a portal to an estuary, about a mile in width, with an enormous perimeter, capacious enough to shelter the Navies of the World. A vessel making the port sails in a few moments out of the long swell of the ocean into calm deep water, protected on every side by high lands. On entering, a splendid vista is presented to our voyager; the elevated shore being broken into innumerable bays and inlets, and the central expanse of water relieved by many a picturesque islet. The rocky shore on each side stretches from heights of above 200 feet down to the water's edge, disclosing at intervals in the distance the white sandy beach of a bay which Stanfield or Copley Fielding would have loved to paint. The well-wooded hills, clothed in the bright garb of spring, or in the russet of summer, and bathed in the glorious light of an Australian atmosphere, form a charming margin to the bright blue waters they enclose. As the city is approached, pretty villas and imposing mansions, surrounded with gardens and orchards, crown the heights or extend along the shore. About four miles from the entrance to the port, and at a point where the southern shore presents several prominent headlands leading to capacious land-locked basins, the city rises into view. It occupies an area of something more than 2,000 acres, and is bounded on the north and west by water. Its greatest length is $3\frac{1}{4}$ miles north and south, and its greatest breadth $2\frac{7}{8}$ miles east and west. It has about 115 miles of streets, irrespective of minor thoroughfares, and numbers 14,500 houses. The population (including the suburbs) is about 140,000; and the funds dispensed by the Corporation last year amounted to about £200,000. Architecturally, Sydney has made rapid strides within the last ten or fifteen years; and its fine banking-houses, mercantile establishments, and handsome public edifices, give it an aspect bespeaking substantial wealth, advancing cultivation and enterprise. The portion convenient, though not close, to the quays, which, as usual in other great seaports, is the most frequented, contains many of the best buildings for commercial purposes; the banks and most of the warehouses being constructed of freestone, in the modern style of Italian composite, and displaying in their façades much rich ornamentation. The grandest specimens of architecture are the University, with its affiliated Colleges, the New Post Office, the Town Hall, the Museum, and Government House, the Anglican and Roman Catholic Cathedrals, and the Churches of Presbyterian, Wesleyan, and Congregational bodies. The private residences in the neighbourhood of Sydney are of a superior character, and are generally in the vicinity of beautiful recreation grounds. The fashionable quarter par excellence is the east end of the city, and the suburban localities stretching thence along the shore. Here are most of those splendid mansions of which glimpses are caught from the harbour, which they overlook. Many of them have been erected at great cost, and for extent, tastefulness of internal decorations, and beauty of their grounds and gardens, are perhaps unequalled by any private residences on this side the equator.

"Although Sydney has few reserves analogous to the squares of London, it has excellent parks and gardens within its boundaries, easily accessible to the citizens. Hyde Park is a beautiful plateau of 40 acres, nearly in the centre of the city. It has a fine avenue about half a mile long, and is nearly surrounded by plantations and clumps of trees, affording a grateful shade, and forming an agreeable resort. The Domain, a charming expanse of park land of 138 acres, planted for landscape effect, is on the north-eastern side of Sydney, surrounding the pretty inlet called Farm Cove. The grounds present every variety required to produce picturesque views, and the artistic disposition of the groups and avenues of trees is fast developing the beauties of this favorite promenade. Near the main entrance is an excellent bronze statue of Sir Richard Bourke, by Baily, in a situation from which is obtained one of the most beautiful views imaginable. The Botanic Gardens embrace 38 acres, and are the finest in the Australian Colonies, for, in addition to the immense collection of exotics from every clime, the site strikes every beholder with admiration.

" More recently formed reserves are Prince Alfred Park and Belmore Park in the south, and a tract of 500 acres on the south-east side, named Moore Park. Adjoining the latter ground is the metropolitan Racecourse, where large fields of horses of the finest breeds, compete at the two half-yearly meetings for stakes which amount to £14,000 or £15,000 in the year.

"The harbour of Port Jackson proper has an area of 9 square miles. Middle Harbour, one of its arms, 3 square miles; and the coast line of the whole is 54 miles. From the heads to the city the distance is 4 miles, beyond which the waters extend 8 miles into what is called the Parramatta River, giving 15 miles as the length of navigation. The average breadth of the navigable waters is three-quarters of a mile, though at some points they widen to 2 miles or more. The shallowest part is between Middle Head and George's Head, where the soundings show 23 feet at low water. Beyond this the depth ranges between 5 and 18 fathoms. There are 3 miles of wharf frontage in use, and about 25 miles of deep water frontage in sheltered places that may be made available for a like purpose.

"The following is the number and tonnage of steam-vessels owned in Sydney, trading to and from the various inland ports and Colonies:—

	Number of vessels.	Horse-power.	Tonnage.
A. S. N. Company	30	3,517	13,464
Clarence and Richmond River Company	15	864	2,786
Illawarra Steam Navigation Company	5	489	1,158
Hunter River New Steam Company	4	480	1,829
Parramatta River Company	4	150	632
Bulli Coal Company	2	80	744
Colonial Sugar Company	3	134	136
Tug-boats	13	745	1,454
Private owned steamers	5	249	830
Passengers and ferry boats	18	336	481

XII.—RAILWAYS, ROADS, AND TELEGRAPHS.

The emigrant who chooses New South Wales as his future home, will find that he has cast in his lot with a people whose energy and civilization is abreast of the age, who have constructed the most gigantic bridges across wide rivers, and carried railways over miles of rugged mountain country, to connect the fertile soil and rich mineral lands of the interior with the sea-board. A population numbering little more than half a million souls has spent £6,653,413 upon railways, £212,255 in making telegraphs; and, during the last ten years, they have expended £2,566,000 on common roads, £675,497 in improving harbours and rivers, and £820,540 in erecting public buildings.

The results of the expenditure of this £10,927,714 are 396½ miles of first-class railway, 6,114 miles of telegraphs, nearly 10,000 miles of common roads cleared (much of the length fenced and also macadamized), courts of justice, hospitals, and other public buildings in all the principal towns of the Colony, lighthouses, break-waters, and wharfs almost wherever they are required.

The amount voted for public works in 1872 was £642,856; and this is about the amount voted by Parliament every year for public improvements out of current revenue. In addition to that, the Government propose to borrow £2,531,280 for railway construction and other public works, the loan to be secured on the Revenues of the Colony.

The northern line of railway starts from the sea-board at Newcastle, and has now reached Murrurundi, 120 miles; and it is intended to extend it to Tamworth, 60¼ miles farther north. The western and southern lines start from Sydney. The former is within five miles of Bathurst (145 miles from Sydney), and is to be extended to Orange, 46½ miles farther west. The southern line is opened to Goulburn (132 miles from Sydney), and is to be extended to Wagga Wagga, 174¼ miles farther. The total length of these extensions, which are to be entered upon at once, is 281 miles; and if care be taken in the selection of contractors and an abundant supply of labour be obtainable, it will be possible to complete the lines to Tamworth, Orange and Yass in two years, and the remaining section of the southern line (that from Yass to Wagga Wagga) in one year more. The Government also intend to construct a line from Grafton to the table-land of New England, to take the traffic westward as far as Glen Innes and Inverell, and northward as far as Tenterfield and the Queensland border.

Railway travelling in New South Wales is almost as rapid and quite as sumptuous as in England. The price of a second-class ticket from Sydney to Goulburn is 28s. 6d., first-class 36s. 2d. A ton of agricultural produce is carried the same distance (132 miles) for 17s. 6d., and of ores, metals, stone, &c., for 26s. 4d. The rates for other descriptions of goods are 29s. 7d., 32s. 10d., 45s. 8d., 56s. 7d., 78s. 5d., and 101s. 3d., according to the classification. The highest rates are for gunpowder, &c. In 1872 our railways carried 753,910 passengers (exclusive of season ticket holders) and 825,317 tons of goods. The total earnings were £425,058.

Telegrams consisting of ten words are sent to any part of the Colony, say from Sydney to Wentworth (835 miles) for 2s. (the rate will be reduced to 1s. in October next), and to England for £10. There are ninety-two telegraph stations in the Colony;

and 335,822 messages were transmitted in 1872, producing a revenue of £45,019. Telegrams from England, Europe, and America, are published in the Sydney newspapers daily, so that the colonists are probably informed earlier of the state of the markets, and of European politics, than the residents of many English towns.

XIII.—POSTAL ARRANGEMENTS.

The Mail Steamer leaves Sydney for Southampton every four weeks, and *vice versa*, and the letters are delivered with wonderful regularity every 56 days. Proposals are under consideration for two other routes, in addition to that which now exists *viâ* Suez, namely :—Sydney to Brisbane and *viâ* Torres Straits, rounding the north of the Continent to Singapore, connecting us directly with India, China Japan, and what we still call the "East." This line is chiefly projected in the interest of Queensland. The other line will run straight across the Pacific from Sydney to San Francisco, across the North American Continent to New York, and over the Atlantic to Liverpool, a service which has once been performed in 47 days. Both these services will probably be established before the end of the year.

At the present time (February, 1873), the Chief Ministers of Victoria, South Australia, Western Australia, Queensland, Tasmania, and New Zealand, are in Sydney, and, with the Premier and Postmaster General of this Colony, are conferring together in respect to Postal Subsidies. In reply to a Minute by the Hon. Henry Parkes (Chief Secretary of New South Wales), dated 10th August, 1872, Lord Kimberley, in a despatch just received by the Governor of the Colony, makes the following concession :— " I have to inform you that Her Majesty's Government will be willing to give their assistance in effecting arrangements for the regular transmission of mails to and from Australasia, through the United States, and that no objection will be raised to the Colonies entering into direct postal conventions with the United States, provided that such conventions are submitted to Her Majesty's Government for final sanction." The Government has obtained Parliamentary authority to send a special Commissioner to the United States Government to negotiate.

In the Colony itself there were, at the close of 1872, 623 post offices. The extent of the postal route was 14,673 miles, the number of miles travelled 3,252,888, and the total cost of conveying the mails, &c., was £87,350, exclusive of the annual vote of £20,000, the subsidy for the conveyance of the European mails by the P. & O. Co's. steamships. The total revenue of the department was £96,477. The number of letters which passed through the Post Office in 1872 was 8,043,200; packets, 135,800; and newspapers, 4,171,500. Letters may be sent to any place 10 miles distant from Sydney for 1d., and to any part of the Colony beyond that distance for 2d., to any of the Australian Colonies and New Zealand for 3d., and to the United Kingdom for 6d. Newspapers go anywhere for a penny, and a Bill has passed the Legislative Assembly to carry them through the Colony free of charge, but failed to pass in the Council.

Money Orders.

The Money Order System is engrafted upon the Post Office. By means of this system any person can send £5 through the Post Office for 6d., or £10 for a shilling; and the regulations are such that fraud is made impossible. The number of money orders issued in 1872 was 87,434, and the value of them £393,862. The system is also extended to all the Australian Colonies and the United Kingdom, the rates of commission being somewhat higher.

Savings Banks.

Government Savings Banks are another valuable adjunct of the Post Office. Sums of 1s. or any multiple of 1s., may be deposited with the Postmaster of the Colony, and the Government pays interest upon the deposits at the rate of four per cent. per annum. The regulations in this department also render peculation impossible. The system has not long been in operation; but the number of depositors in 1872 was 3,226; the total deposits to the 31st December, 1872, £109,343. However remote a man may be from the large towns, he has all the advantages of a high civilization and good government extended to him.

XIV.—LABOUR AND WAGES.

There is a great demand for labour of all kinds in the Colony, but more particularly is there a demand for it in agricultural and mining pursuits. Two or three columns of the daily newspapers are every morning devoted to making known the wants of employers of all kinds, and a considerable space is occupied by the advertisements for servants who can be hired for neither love nor money. Of 800 emigrants who came out to the Colony by Government assistance, the great majority of them being single women, none died on the voyage, and *all obtained engagements in respectable families immediately they landed*, the rates of wages being from £20 to £22 6s. 6d. per annum. The Immigration Agent says: "A much larger number than have already arrived would readily obtain situations as domestic servants." The prospects of unskilled labourers may be judged of from what has been already written. They may reckon upon obtaining from 6s. to 8s., per day; and, in addition to the ordinary demands of the Country, this fact is worth remembering:—*The Government are about to spend two millions sterling in making railways and constructing other public works* within the next two years.

The appended list shows the rates of wages in the principal departments of labour ruling in January, 1873:—

THE IRON TRADES.

Engine-fitters, 7s. 6d. to 12s. 6d. per day
„ turners, 10s. to 12s. 6d.
Pattern-makers, 8s. 4d. to 12s.
Moulders (iron), 8s. 4d. to 12s. 1d.
„ (brass), 10s. to 12s. 6d.
Blacksmiths, 8s. 4d. to 14s.
Boiler-makers, 8s. 4d. to 14s.
Copper and general smiths, 8s. 4d. to 11s. 8d.
Riveters, 6s. 8d. to 10s.
Fitters, 8s. 4d. to 11s. 8d.
Strikers, 5s. 10d. to 10s.
Assistants (boiler-makers), 6s. 8d. to 8s. 4d.
Assistants (blacksmiths), 5s. 10d. to 7s. 6d.
Furnace men, 8s. 4d. to 10s.
Brass-finishers, 9s.
Labourers, 5s. 10d. to 7s.
Engine-drivers, 6s. 8d. to 7s. 1d.
„ (railway), 10s. to 14s.
Firemen „ 7s. to 10s.

BUILDING TRADES.

Plumbers, 10s. per day.
Carpenters and joiners, 8s. to 10s.
Painters, 9s.
Masons, 10s.
Bricklayers, 9s. to 10s.
Sawyers, 8s. 4d. to 10s.
Labourers, 8s. to 8s. 6d.

COACH AND CARRIAGE BUILDERS.

Smiths, 7s. 6d. to 10s.
Wheel-makers, 7s. 6d. to 10s.
Body-makers, 8s. 4d. to 11s. 8d.
Painters, 8s. 4d. to 10s. 10d.
Trimmers, 8s. 4d. to 10s.

MINERS.

Gold, 50s. to 60s. per week.
Tin, 42s. „ 50s. „
Copper, 50s. „ 60s. „
Coal, 50s. „ 80s. „

SHIPWRIGHTS.

Old work, 12s.
New work, 11s.

RAILWAY CARRIAGE BUILDERS.

Carpenters and joiners, 10s. to 11s. 8d. per day.
Carriage-builders, 8s. 4d. to 13s. 4d.
„ trimmers, 8s. 4d. to 13s. 4d.
„ painters, 8s. 4d. to 13s. 4d.
Machine men and sawyers, 6s. 10d. to 11s. 8d.

LEATHER TRADES.

Tanners, 6s. 8d. to 9s. 2d. per day.
Curriers, 8s. 4d. to 11s. 8d.
Bootmakers, 6s. 8d. to 11s. 8d.
Machine hands (girls), 1s. 8d. to 5s.

IN THE COUNTRY.

The following quotations include board and lodging, or hut room and rations, per annum:—
Carpenters and blacksmiths, £50 to £70.
Rough carpenters, £40 to £50.
Married farm and domestic servants, £50 to £60.
Grooms and gardeners, £40 to £50.
Farm and garden labourers, £30 to £35.
Surveyor's men and bushmen, £35 to £40.
Ploughmen, stockmen, and shepherds, £35 to £40.
Boys for farms and stations, £18 to £20.
Female servants, £20 to £30.

IN THE TOWNS.

Cooks, 12s. to 15s. per week.
Housemaids, 10s. to 12s.
Laundresses, 12s. to 16s.
Nursemaids, 8s. to 12s.
General house servants, 10s. to 12s.
Governesses, £26 to £100 per annum.
Housekeepers, £35 to £150 ditto.

Millers, £3 a week.
Draymen, £2 2s. to £2 5s. ditto
Coopers, £2 to £3 10s.

XV.—THE COST OF LIVING.

FOOD AND HOUSE-RENT.

Persons who have small fixed incomes, and to whom the cost of living is an object, cannot do better than emigrate to New South Wales, where they may enjoy all the advantages of European civilization, at the most moderate cost. For such, the Colony is a most desirable place of residence, since here they may enjoy life under the happiest and most favoured conditions, and may find a congenial sphere for the activity of all their interests and sympathies. But specific information is better than generalization. The following is the official list of prices in the Sydney markets. In the country, things are quite as cheap, for there people grow their own fruit and vegetables, make their own butter and cheese, cure their own bacon, and feed their own poultry; or, if too indolent to surround themselves with these comforts of rural life, they can buy them at a cheap rate, or accept the only other alternative—go without.

SYDNEY MARKETS, JANUARY 31, 1873.

The Mills.

	Wholesale.	Retail.
Bakers' silk-dressed flour, per ton of 2,000 lbs.	£14.	
Fine, per ditto	£13.	
Seconds ditto, ditto	£12.	
Bran, per bushel	1s.	
Biscuit, cabin, per 100 lbs.	24s.	
Navy, ditto	16s.	
Bread, per 2-lb. loaf	—	3d. to 4½d.

Butchers' Meat.

Beef, per lb.	2¼d. to 2½d.	2½d. to 5d.
Mutton, per ditto	2¼d. to 2½d.	2½d. to 5d.
Pork, per ditto	4d. to 5d.	5d. to 7d.
Veal, per ditto	4d.	4½d. to 6d.
Lamb, per quarter	3s. 6d. to 4s.	4s. to 5s.

Poultry.

Fowls, per couple	2s. 6d. to 3s.	3s. to 4s.
Ducks, per ditto	2s. 9d. to 3s.	3s. 3d. to 4s. 6d.
Geese, per ditto	5s. to 8s.	8s. to 12s.
Turkeys, per ditto	6s. to 20s.	8s. to 25s.
Pigeons, per ditto	1s. to 1s. 6d.	1s. 6d. to 2s. 6d.
Rabbits, per pair	2s. to 2s. 6d.	2s. 6d. to 4s.
Roasting pigs, each	3s. 6d. to 4s. 6d.	4s. to 6s.

Dairy Produce.

Butter, per lb.	3d. to 5d.	6d. to 9d.
Cheese, per ditto	2d. to 4½d.	4d. to 8d.
Bacon, per ditto	5d. to 6½d.	6d. to 9d.
Lard, per ditto	5d.	7d.
Eggs, per dozen	4d. to 6d.	7d. to 10d.

Vegetables.

Potatoes, per cwt.	3s. to 4s.	4s. to 5s.
Onions, per ditto	3s. to 4s.	2d. lb.
Cabbages, per dozen	1s. to 3s.	2d. to 6d. each
Lettuces, per ditto	6d. to 1s.	2d.
Pumpkins, per ditto	3s. to 6s.	3d. to 9d.
Marrows, per ditto	2s. to 3s.	3d. to 6d.
Cucumbers, per ditto	6d. to 1s.	1d. to 2d.
Turnips, per dozen bunches	1s. 6d. to 2s. 6d.	3d.
Carrots, per ditto ditto	1s. to 1s. 6d.	2d.

NEW SOUTH WALES. 89

Parsnips, per ditto ditto	1s. to 1s. 6d.	2d. to 3d.
Beetroot, per ditto ditto	—	2d. to 3d.
Leeks, per ditto ditto............	—	1d. to 2d. each
Rhubarb, per ditto ditto	1s. to 2s.	2d. to 3d.
Celery, per ditto ditto	—	3d. to 6d. per head
Green pease, per bushel..........	4s. to 6s.	2s. to 2s. 6d. per peck
French beans, per ditto..........	1s. to 1s. 6d.	6d. to 7d.

Fruit.

Oranges, per case	5s. to 12s.	5d. to 2s. 6d. per doz.
Lemons, per ditto	10s.	1s. to 2s.
Apples, per ditto....................	2s. to 6s.	2d. to 1s. 6d.
Nectarines, per ditto	2s. 6d. to 3s. 6d.	2d. to 6d.
Pears, per ditto	2s. 6d. to 3s.	2d. to 6d.
Peaches, per ditto	1s. 6d. to 2s. 6d.	2d. to 8d.
Plums, per ditto...................	3s. 6d. to 4s.	2d. to 6d. per quart
Greengages, per ditto............	6s. to 7s.	3d. to 6d. per dozen
Pineapples, per dozen	1s. 6d. to 2s. 6d.	
Water melons, per ditto	3s.	4d. to 1s. each
Rock ditto, per ditto	3s. to 4s.	3d. to 1s.
Passion-fruit, per ditto	1d.	2d. to 3d. per dozen
Bananas, per ditto	3d. to 6d.	6d. to 9d.
Grapes, per lb.	2d. to 3½d.	4d. to 8d. per lb.
Honey, per ditto..................	3d.	4d. to 6d.

Forage.

Straw, per cwt.	4s. 10d. to 5s. 3d.
Lucerne, per ditto	2s. 5d. to 2s. 10d.
Oaten, per ditto	5s. to 7s.
Maize, per bushel	1s. 8d. to 1s. 10d.
Oats, per ditto	2s. 6d. to 3s. 9d.
Barley, per ditto..................	3s.
Wheat, per ditto	4s. 6d. to 4s. 9d.
Green food, per dozen bundles	6d. to 8d.

House-rent is somewhat higher in Sydney than in most of the large towns of England. But a very considerable proportion of the population live in their own houses; and any labouring man, artisan, clerk, or shopman, can, by paying a small sum weekly, equivalent to (say) 25 per cent. of his earnings, into one or other of the Building Societies, become his own landlord in the course of eight or ten years. If a man does not choose to buy his house in this way, he will have to make a deduction of 20 per cent. from his wages for house-rent.

PROVISIONS AND CLOTHING.

The following Return, showing "the average price of Provisions and Clothing in Sydney, for the year 1871," is copied from the last volume of the Statistical Register.

Articles of consumption.	Quantity.	Price.	Articles of clothing.	Quantity.	Price.
Wheat	bushel	5s. 10.	Moleskin jackets	each	10s. 6d.
Bread, first quality	lb.	2d.	Do. coats	,,	13s.
Do. second do.	,,	1½d.	Waistcoats	,,	4s. 6d.
Flour, first quality	,,	14s. per 100 lbs.	Moleskin trousers	per pair	6s.
Do. second do.	,,	12s. per do.	Coloured shirts	each	3s. 6d.
Rice	,,	2¼d.	Strong boots	per pair	5s. 6d.
Oatmeal	,,	2¼d.	Do. shoes	,,	4s. 6d.
Tea	,,	1s. 9d to 2s. 6d.	Shepherds' coats	each	15s.
Sugar	,,	3½d. to 4½d.	Socks	per pair	9d.
Coffee	,,	1s.	Handkerchiefs, cotton.	each	6d.
Sago	,,	3d.			
Meat, fresh	,,	2¼d.	Straw hats	,,	2s. 6d.
Do. salt	,,	1¼d.			
Butter, fresh	,,	1s. 3d.	*Female Clothing.*		
Do. salt	,,	1s.	Print dresses	each	7s.
Cheese, English	,,	1s.	Merino	,,	10s.
Do. Colonial	,,	6d. to 9d.	Flannel petticoats	,,	5s. 6d.
Salt	,,	0½d.	Calico do.	,,	7d.
Potatoes	cwt.	4s.	Stockings	per pair	1s. 8d.
Wine, Colonial	gallon	2s. 6d. to 8s. 6d.	Shoes	,,	3s. 9d.
Beer, Colonial	,,	1s. 9d. to 2s. 9d.	Shawls	each	8s.
Candles, tallow	lb.	5d.	Check aprons	,,	1s.
Kerosene oil	gallon	3s.	Straw bonnets	,,	2s.
Soap	lb.	3d.	Flannel	per yard	2s. 0d.
Tobacco, Colonial	,,	1s.	Calico	,,	7d.
			Bedding.		
			Blankets	per pair	9s.
			Sheeting, calico	per yard	2s. 3d.
			Mattresses	each	15s. to 30s.
			Rugs	,,	6s. 9d.

XVI.—EDUCATION, LITERATURE, AND RELIGION.

An ignorant people never thrives. Throughout the World well-informed and intelligent nations are coming to the front, and the uneducated and illiterate are falling into the back ground. The two peoples that have made the most rapid progress in all the elements of national strength during the last twenty years are probably the Americans and the Germans, and they are proverbially the best educated peoples of modern times. The Prussian Public School system did more to transform Prussia into Germany than all the elaborate military organization of Frederick the Great. While these nations were sowing the seeds of knowledge broadcast among their subjects, England was muddling away immense sums of money in educating the upper and middle classes in her Universities and endowed schools, leaving the children of the people to the mercy of desultory individual effort and sectarian prejudice. But the extension of political privileges has forced upon her rulers some scheme of national education; for it is a duty which the State owes to itself to see to it that those whose suffrages are to determine its future should be able to give an intelligent vote. In the emphatic words of Horace Mann, in a self-governing community "ignorance is a crime; and private immorality is not less an opprobrium to the State than it is guilt in the perpetrator."

The youth of New South Wales saves her from this sad inheritance of ignorance and misery to which millions in Europe are born. In 1848 Government began to give large sums of money for the purposes of primary instruction, to the two Boards of Education—the National and the Denominational; but in 1866 the Public Schools Act was passed, sweeping away both Boards, and making Education a department of the State; administered by a Council of Education, consisting of five members nominated by the Governor, and responsible to the Executive Council, like all other branches of the Public Service. The Act provides for the establishment of Public Schools wherever, in the judgment of the Council, they may be needed, and for the maintenance of Certified Denominational Schools, under certain conditions. But all schools supported by the State must be under Government inspection, the teachers must be examined and certified by the Council, and the same course of secular instruction must be adopted, all class books used being subject to Government approbation. Under this system education is spreading as fast as the population; every town and considerable village has its school; itinerant teachers are even appointed to visit the families of settlers scattered through the bush; and it is the policy of the Colony to leave no place in all the land where ignorance may hide and social misery fester, to become a curse to the community.

There is a school fee charged usually amounting to one shilling per week; but a reduction is made where several children attend from the same family; and, in every case where the parents are unable to pay the fee, education is free of charge.

The salaries of the teachers vary from £72 to £150 per annum from Government, in addition to the school fees, which are divided ratably among the teachers in large schools, and not uncommonly more than double the salary.

The standards of proficiency begin with children over five years old in the first class, who are examined by the Inspector in reading, writing, arithmetic, and singing, and advance to the fifth class, including reading, writing, arithmetic, grammar, geography, object lessons, singing, drawing, geometry, algebra, and Latin, with permission to teachers to produce, if possible, higher results. While the chief aim of the Council is to make elementary instruction universal, it is also intended to rectify as far as possible the inequalities of fortune, and put it within the power of the poorest family in the land to obtain a thoroughly liberal education.

There are now 878 schools existing under the new Act, with 87,313 children on the rolls, of whom 7,069 are taught free of charge. The number of teachers is 1,225; the amount of school fees, £43,503; local contributions to buildings, £3,404; from public funds, £113,158; total, £160,065. Many of the middle classes avail themselves of the excellent facilities of the Public Schools for the education of their children, deeming them more efficient than any other at their command; and regarding it as a good thing that all the children of the Country should start life from this common educational platform. But there are in the Colony 561 private schools, with 826 teachers—many of them are graduates of Universities; and with an attendance of 13,700 children. Altogether, 101,000 children are enrolled in the public and private schools of the Colony—more than one-fifth of the entire population. Besides these, there are Mechanics' Institutes and Schools of Arts established in most of the leading towns, to which Government contributes a sum equal to that raised by local voluntary subscriptions and donations. There are also numerous prizes and scholarships available for all who distinguish themselves at the Public Examination of the University, by means of which the poorest child may receive a University training free of expense.

The University of Sydney was established and endowed in 1851. In its constitution it approaches somewhat to University College, London, with the power of granting degrees in arts, law, and medicine, and with a guaranteed annual income from the public funds of £5,000. Last year it had six Professors, with 18 additional Examiners for degrees, 141 graduates, and 45 students. Its fundamental principle is the association of students, without respect of religious creeds, in the cultivation of secular knowledge. But, as in the case of the University of London, provision is made for Affiliated Colleges of the different religious denominations, with an additional guarantee from the public funds of one-half the cost of building each college, where the denomination has contributed the other half, and £500 per annum towards the salary of each Principal when duly elected. Under these provisions, St. Paul's Church of England College and St. John's Roman Catholic College are already in existence, and two more are projected in connection with the Presbyterian and Wesleyan bodies. By glancing over these facts, the reader will perceive that the Colony has a complete system of educational institutions, adapted to its wants, and capable of expanding with its growth to the proportion of the most colossal Empire. In regard to the literary condition of the people, it is perhaps enough for the purposes of this pamphlet simply to state that the Colony has eighty-four newspapers—many of them published twice and thrice a week, besides the daily, weekly, and monthly Sydney Press; periodicals, with a circulation varying from a few hundred up to 15,000; that in the capital there are three public libraries, numbering about 60,000 volumes, and taking in all the leading English, American, and many Foreign periodicals; that many thousands per annum are spent in importing English periodical literature, and not less than £50,000 per annum in imported books, and that a native literature has been created, consisting already of several hundred volumes, in all departments of literature and science, some of which have been favourably reviewed by the leading journals of Europe and America, and are standard works on the subjects of which they treat. The Municipalities Act empowers the Borough Councils to establish free libraries; and if the library be established in a district where 300 persons can regularly make use of it the Council is entitled to a grant of £100 from the General Revenue, and £200 if within reach of 1,000 souls. Several libraries have already been established, and others are projected. Of the religious condition of the people, little need be said here beyond the statement that all the leading religious denominations of England are efficiently represented; that there is perfect religious equality, that direct State-aid to Religion was abolished by Act of Parliament in the year 1862, provision being made for the existing life interests, so that the payments are now reduced to £22,976, and are being still further reduced year by year as the selected lives fall in. The number of registered ministers of all denominations is 501, the number of churches and chapels is 924, the accommodation provided in them is for 181,914, and the average attendance 176,596. The number of Sunday Schools in the Colony is 933, with 6,049 teachers, and some 60,000 scholars. The following table of the Religion of the people, taken from the Census of 1871, may perhaps give the best idea of the status of the different denominations:—

Church of England	229,243	
Presbyterians	49,122	
Wesleyan Methodists	36,275	
Other Methodists	3,291	
Congregationalists	9,253	
Baptists	4,151	
Unitarians	849	
Protestants undescribed	2,549	
Other Protestants	4,659	
Total Protestants		339,392
Roman Catholics	145,932	
Catholics undescribed	1,695	
Total Catholics		147,627
Hebrews	2,395	
Other Persuasions	1,166	
Pagans	7,455	
Unspecified	5,946	
Total		16,962
Total Population		503,981

XVII.—SOCIAL CONDITION OF THE PEOPLE.

Wealth has no value except as the means of promoting the comfort and happiness of the people. For this reason the nation which has the largest aggregate of wealth may be far from being the happiest, for its wealth may be accumulated in the hands of a few, while the masses of the people remain in abject poverty. Every man, whether rich or poor, has a right to the free use of all his faculties and opportunities, and to those social rewards which the circumstances of the land in which he dwells may secure him; but the most desirable state of prosperity is where the productive powers of the Country are guided by the best laws of distribution, so that all the people, by sobriety and industry, may be well to do. Mr. Mill, in his Principles of Political Economy, says:—" To begin life as hired labourers, then after a few years to work on their own account, and, finally, employ others, is the normal condition of labourers in a new Country rapidly increasing in wealth and population, like America and Australia; but in an old and fully peopled Country, those who begin life as labourers for hire, as a general rule continue such to the end, unless they sink into the still lower grade of recipients of public charity."

In New South Wales pauperism does not exist, and poverty is almost unknown, except as the result of accidents or intemperance. With wages as high as in the United States, and provisions cheaper than in England, and far more varied and abundant, and a most genial and delightful climate, with no rigorous winter to fear, the condition of the working classes is one of greater enjoyment probably than in any other part of the World. How many thousands of families are there in Europe to whom animal meat is a forbidden luxury, or to be obtained only once or twice a week. Here it is to be found on any table every day; and, while consuming four times as much meat per head of the population as in England, we have still available immense consignments of tinned meats, which, after paying the cost of a long voyage and the profits of dealers, can still be sold in the English markets at half the price of butcher's meat. Here, too, the orange, nectarine, peach, grape, apricot, and other choice fruits, which in England are to be found only on the tables of the rich, the produce of hot-house culture, grow under the blue sky to perfection, and any one can furnish his table daily with a liberal dessert at the cost of a few pence.

The means of saving for the industrial classes are as abundant as the comforts of life are plentiful. In Sydney and the leading towns thousands of working men occupy their own houses, and live rent free, by accumulating their savings for a few years in Building Societies. There are 28,787 depositors in the Savings Bank of New South Wales and Post Office Savings Banks. The amount of deposits on 31st December, 1872, was £1,286,193, the rate of interest allowed being 4 and 5 per cent. There are several Building Societies and branches in the Colony, one of which—the Permanent Mutual Benefit Building Society, in Sydney—has 9,371 investing shares taken up, paying 2s. 6d. per month, and has advanced on mortgage to shareholders £76,525, holding other deposits to the amount of £50,540. Other Societies do an almost equal amount of business.

Many of the leading English Friendly Societies have branches here. The Independent Order of Oddfellows, of the Manchester Unity, has 83 lodges in the Colony, 5,593 beneficiary members, an income in 1872 of £27,909, a hall which cost £7,300, and an invested capital of £39,877. An entrance fee of from 12s. to £4, according to age, is first paid, and then from 1s. to 1s. 3d., for which there is an allowance of 21s. per week during illness, with medical attendance for the members of his family, and funeral expenses after death to the extent of £20, to the nearest relative, and from £25 to £50 where there is a widow surviving. There are 42 Hospitals spread all over the Country, and the principal of these—the Sydney Infirmary—in 1871 admitted 1840 patients, and at the close of the year had 232 in residence; its income was £12,792, of which sum £2,527 was from private donations, and £10,265 from Government.

There are six Benevolent Asylums, with 1,572 inmates, and an income for the year of £18,120.

There are eleven Orphan and Industrial Schools. One of these—the Randwick Asylum for Destitute Children—had, at the close of the year, 809 inmates, with an income of £11,954.

There is an Institute for the Deaf and Dumb and the Blind, on the Newtown Road; a fine and extensive structure, with every convenience for the maintenance and instruction of these afflicted fellow-colonists, and with an income of £3,402.

In the Harbour there is a Nautical School for Vagrant Boys, on board the ship "Vernon," and on Biloela Island an Industrial School for Girls, of a similar character; both intended to save these classes from falling into crime and becoming inmates of our prisons.

There is a Sailors' Home, a Female Refuge, and many other similar Institutions, maintained both by private contribution and Government aid. Altogether, for the year 1871, the total income of the Colony for known organized Public Charities of all kinds was £114,841. Nor are the sympathies of the colonists confined within their own bounds, for they contributed to the Crimean Patriotic Fund £64,916; to the Indian Mutiny Fund, £5,821; to the Lancashire Cotton Famine Relief Fund, £21,311.

Of the provident habits of the people the extensive business done by Life Insurance Offices is ample evidence. All the leading English Offices are represented in the Colony; but the most prosperous Office for life business is native—the Australian Mutual Provident Society. It has existed only twenty-two years, yet it has an annual income of about £250,000, and invested funds amounting to nearly £1,000,000. Its scale of premiums is lower than in many of the best English Offices, while its profits up to this year are equal to a cash bonus of 60 per cent. of the total premiums paid.

Of the accumulated wealth of the community, the following facts afford some evidence:—The amount deposited in the Mercantile and Savings Banks in the Colony, on the 31st December, 1872, was £10,411,166. Municipal government was established in 1867, and now, besides the capital, there are forty Boroughs and twenty-one Municipal Districts already existing. The assessed value of rateable property in the Municipality of Sydney—exclusive of its suburbs, is £726,139, and the Corporation spent in 1871, upon City works of various kinds, £141,056. For all other Municipalities in the Colony, exclusive of Sydney, the assessed value of rateable property is £12,243,630. In all the Municipalities the immigrant would find all the institutions, habits, customs, and courtesies of English town life prevailing, except the parish Work-house, and its prevailing causes and effects; schemes of water supply, plans of sewerage, and irrigation, Gas Companies, Schools, Churches, Clubs, Working-men's Institute, and other phases of social life which spring up among self-governing peoples. And all this machinery is worked without disorder; bribery and corruption, even in municipal elections are unknown. Whether the tastes of the settler are for town or country, the Colony can offer him a life thoroughly enjoyable. The city has its public buildings, its University, Clubs, Schools,—able ministers and orators, its Libraries, Parks, Baths, Public Gardens, Pleasure-grounds, all round the harbour, and aquatic sports spread over all the year. The country has its varied recreations; inland lakes abounding with wild fowl, woods swarming with parrots and other birds of gorgeous plumage; plains where coveys of partridges and wild turkeys gratify the sportsman's vanity and reward his skill, with no Game Laws to prevent the humblest labourer from enjoying his share; while on the verge of the Settled Districts, the emu and the noble kangaroo still run and leap over their natural pastures, affording sport to the hunter, the most exhilarating and exciting. Nearly all our city youth can manage a boat fairly, bend the sail and ply the oar, and cast the fishing-line to some purpose; and, attracted by the blue waters of the harbour, nearly all can breast the waves and enjoy a header in the sea. Horses are plentiful and cheap, both to buy and keep, riding is an almost universal accomplishment, and our young bushmen are among the finest riders in the World.

A Public Holiday in Sydney,

Public holidays are frequent, and are observed with peculiar regard, and enjoyed with great gusto all over the Colony. A holiday in Sydney is a sight worth seeing. The weather is almost always fine, and there is no part of the year when out-door amusements are not thoroughly enjoyable. A rigorous winter never interferes with the pleasure-seeker, and though a hot wind sometimes blows in summer, it is seldom indeed that the temperature is at all hot enough to mar the enjoyment of a holiday. Christmas Day here presents a remarkable contrast to Christmas Day in England; and the day after—Boxing Day—is universally observed as a day of festivity; so also is Anniversary Day, the 26th of January. On Queen's Birthday, too, the shops are closed, the warehouses deserted, the factories silent; banners and evergreens adorn the houses; the streets are alive with processions, marching in the early morning, with flags flying and bands playing, down to the harbour, where every steamer of the port has been engaged for the day; bells are ringing, salutes fired from the batteries, and returned from the vessels of war anchored under Government House. Every ship in port, from whatever clime, is decorated with flags of all colours, from stem to stern, from top-mast to hull. Hundreds of yachts dot the blue water, their white sails glittering in the sun; the Regatta has assembled 20,000 spectators, crowding the Flagship, and lining the shores on either side, to watch the swiftest craft built on this side the Equator contend for the prizes offered, and still more for the honor of victory. All round the capacious harbour there are hundreds of beautiful winding bays, affording camping-ground and the most picturesque scenery to pic-nicing parties, who climb the rocks, ascend the summits, play on the sands, bathe in the waters, and practice cricket, croquet, foot-ball, and all the well-known English games, on the soft green sward.

Clontarf is a favourite haunt with the holiday-makers, and is a spot of surpassing beauty. From the foot of George and Pitt Streets in the city, steamers ply all day, steam down the harbour for six miles, cross the opening between the heads, where the heavy swell of the Pacific Ocean rolls in upon the Middle Head, and gives the extremely squeamish stomach just five minutes suggestion of what sea-sickness is, besides affording no small amusement to their more robust friends; and in half an hour from leaving the crowded streets and wharfs of the city, you land on a sylvan spot, where Nature still wears her primeval garb. First, there is the beach of pure white sand, then a large plot of green turf, as smooth as if levelled with the roller, with patches of trees, and seats and tables under them, for the accommodation of the public. Then there is a background of rocks, covered with lichen and moss, and fern, and wooded to the summit, rising almost perpendicularly some 200 feet, and commanding a view of Sydney on one side and of the Pacific Ocean on the other, and the whole harbour at your feet. Here often 10,000 spectators gather to witness all kinds of sports; breaking up into little family knots in all directions, and, with shouts of laughter and the blending of merry voices, doing ample justice to the varied and abundant food with which they have come provided.

Manly Beach, about a mile across the bush from Clontarf, and built on the Pacific on one side, and on another bay of Port Jackson on the other, an interval of but 500 yards separating the two, is another favourite resort; and here often as many thousands more spend the livelong day. Then there is Pearl Bay, Chowder Bay, Athol Gardens, Balmoral, Cremorne, and many similar places on the same side (the North Shore), each vieing with the other in beauty and attractiveness, and all thronged with visitors. A more gorgeous and exhilarating scene than these places present when the blaze of noon is succeeded by the more subdued light of evening, and wood, sky, and sea combine, their charms cannot be imagined. Future poets will find inspiration here for ages, and, in thoughts that breathe and words that burn, immortalize the glories of their native land.

The other side of the harbour has its attractions too. Darling Point, Double Bay, Rose Bay, Watson's Bay, and, not the least, the Domain, and Botanical Gardens—situate within two minutes' walk of the main streets of the city, and yet as rural as if they were miles distant. These Gardens are superb; abounding with magnificent specimens of all the varied vegetation of the Colony, and the choicest productions of the Islands and other lands; tastefully laid out; interspersed with flower-beds and grass-plots, sloping down to a level greensward, where military bands play, and the citizens promenade, while the ripple of the waves is heard at their feet, and the dark foliage of the North Shore bounds the view in the background. Almost perfect judgment has been displayed in the laying out of these grounds, and Nature was lavish in the advantages which she bestowed. No wonder that holidays or working days the citizens never tire of this paradise, and visitors from all parts never grow weary in its praise. Besides these natural pleasure-grounds of the harbour, there are other charming spots on the Pacific coast, within eight miles of the city: Bondi, Coogee, Long Bay, Botany Bay, and many more, to which the people wend in omnibuses, coaches, cabs, vans, and every kind of vehicle which can be pressed into their service. All the roads from the city are crowded with lines of conveyances, and joyous voices are heard singing, laughing, and joining in merry converse all day long. The Albert Cricket Ground, the Rifle Butts, Moore Park, Tempe, Sans Souci, and a score of other places, all present their temptations and attract their patrons; while Government puts on extra trains at half-fare to bring the country population to the capital, and give the inhabitants of the city an opportunity of tasting the reality of country life and seeing the grand wild scenery of the Blue Mountains. Altogether, we believe it is no boast, but the simple truth to declare that there is not another spot known to civilized man combining in itself such a variety of attractions for the recreation of its people as this capital of New South Wales; and it is estimated that at least three-fourths of the whole population turn out to enjoy these holidays, and return home refreshed, reinvigorated, orderly, and sober, to resume the serious business of life all the more vigorously next day. And though so many assemble on the various places, they never seem crowded; they are numerous and vast enough to afford secluded nooks and corners to all who love quietness, even where the largest numbers go there for the day. All appear well dressed, well provided with the most liberal and even luxurious fare, perfectly well conducted, contented and happy. Drunkenness is seldom seen, and riots and general disorder never. Occasionally overcrowding on the piers to get on board the steamers will tumble one or two into the water, but there are always good swimmers ready to plunge after them, and the only inconvenience suffered is an unexpected cold bath, and the necessity for a change of dress. A whole year's holidays commonly pass and not a life is lost in all the hundreds of excursions. One or two policemen are in attendance at each chief pic-nicing place, but commonly the only service they have to perform is to hand the little ones over the vessel's side, or occasionally fish an unlucky wight out of the water, and to their credit be it said, that this service they are always ready to perform. Civility and good manners in a pushing crowd are somewhat rare, but nowhere are they less rare than in these holiday-makings of the inhabitants of Sydney.

XVIII.—HINTS TO EMIGRANTS.

1. Do not bring a large stock of miscellaneous articles, in the belief that you will find them dearer here. Look over the list of prices given in these pages. Add to the Home price the cost of carriage and freight from England, allow for the risks of the voyage, and the encumbrance of moving with much luggage, and then select very judiciously such things as you find most suitable to your condition and intentions. As a rule, the less luggage the better, for nothing is more useful here than money.

2. For the voyage, unless you are prepared to rough it somewhat, it is better, especially if you have a family, to bring a case or two of selected provisions in your cabin. The best ships are well and liberally provisioned; they have their regular hours for meals, and as a rule supper is not one of their institutions. A good supply of cheap clothing is desirable, very light for the tropics, and as warm as for winter in England, as ships run up to 42° sometimes, and always as high as 38°, where it is sure to be tolerably cold.

3. Emigrant ships chartered by the Government of New South Wales are occasionally sent out. For all particulars respecting these, apply to the Agent-General of New South Wales, at present Sir Charles Cowper, 3 Westminster Chambers, London, S.W., who is instructed, on behalf of the Colony, to supply all information and advice gratis to intending emigrants, and who will render you every assistance in his power.

4. If you do not come by an emigrant ship, choose one belonging to a house of good standing and in the regular trade, as outsiders sometimes run at less fares, but with wretched accommodation. The prices for a passage to Sydney are £40 to £50 first class, £25 to £30 second class, and £16 to £20 third class. The length of the voyage varies from 74 to 100 days. The leading shipping houses to Sydney are Messrs. Devitt & Moore, 109 Leadenhall-street, London, and their regular liners are the "Parramatta," "Sobraon," "Commissary," "Hawkesbury," "Bruckley Castle," "Windsor Castle," "Agnes Rose," "Ben Lomond," "Alexander Duthie," "Rifleman," "Dunbar Castle," &c. Messrs. Geo. Thompson & Co., 24 Leadenhall-street, is another of the leading shipping firms, and among the vessels which they despatch regularly to Sydney are the "Patriarch," "Christiana Thompson," "Ethiopian," "Kósciusko," "Ascalon," "Damascus," "Nineveh," &c. Messrs. Holder, Bros. & Co. are also in the trade, and their offices are at 146 Leadenhall-street, London.

5. Passengers have to furnish their own cabins, and care should be taken to have the berths firmly fixed before leaving the dock. Mattresses made to fit the berths, and good enough for the voyage, can be had for a few shillings at any respectable dealers close by the Docks in London. Other articles required, such as blankets, sheets, pillows, basins for washing, water-can, &c., will be equally useful on landing. A few books should be provided for reading, or materials for sewing, to prevent time hanging heavily on your hands. Be sure to close the window of your cabin at night if there is the slightest sign of wind; and have a sufficient supply of the cheapest underclothing you can get, to last the whole voyage, as washing is not always convenient at sea.

6. If, on landing at Sydney, you want advice or information, go to the Immigration Depôt at Hyde Park. It is maintained by the Government, and there you will be able to get trustworthy information about wages and employment, the situation of different districts, modes of travelling, means of taking up land, and everything else of importance to the settler. The intemperate and the idle need not apply, as this institution is not a charity, but a means of protecting *bona fide* immigrants from extortion and imposition.

XIX.—SUMMARY OF THE ADVANTAGES OF NEW SOUTH WALES AS A HOME FOR THE EMIGRANT.

1. There is ready employment for all classes of labourers and artisans, at double the wages given to the same classes of labour in England.

2. The cost of living for the masses of the people is cheaper here than at Home. The necessaries and common comforts of life are cheaper. Some of the luxuries are dearer; but fruits of all varieties are most abundant and exceedingly cheap. The labouring classes throughout the Colony are as well fed, as well clothed, and live as comfortably as the middle classes in England.

3. Capital finds ready investment either in trade, agriculture, mining, or the public stock, at much higher rates than in Europe, and with as good security. Eight per cent. with good security is deemed a fair rate in Sydney; in the country, rates run higher.

4. There is an area of nearly 200,000,000 acres of public lands, two-thirds of which are occupied by the squatters on short leases, but all of which are open to the emigrant to select from, wherever he pleases, and on terms within reach of the poorest, and a certain road to wealth, if he be healthy, prudent, and industrious.

5. The soil and climate are adapted to every variety of produce, at the least expenditure of labour and capital; and, cultivated with the same skill as at Home, will yield far better returns.

6. Our mineral resources can be surpassed by no other Country. The gold deposits are spread over a larger area, and are proving richer than anything hitherto known in the whole history of mining. The coal deposits are inexhaustible, and copper, tin, kerosene shale, and other mineral treasures abound.

7. For merchants and tradesmen no fairer field than Sydney could be presented. Its position on the eastern seaboard, with the Southern Islands, San Francisco, and the whole American Continent, right opposite,—with a harbour for shipping unrivalled in the World, and a vast trade already established, it cannot fail to secure the chief share of the commerce of the Pacific.

8. No finer climate can be desired, alike free from the rigorous cold of England, Canada, and the North-western States of America, and from the enervating heat of India and the tropics.

9. In natural scenery, New South Wales can vie with some of the romantic Countries of Europe. The wild picturesque scenery of the Blue Mountains, and the manifold beauty of Port Jackson, the glorious landscapes of New England, the Clarence, Monaro, Illawarra, and other parts, cannot well be surpassed.

10. Every district is easy of access by river, road, or railway. The most formidable barrier, long thought impassable, has been crossed by a Railway, along which passengers and produce are carried day and night, in carriages as comfortable as any in Europe. The whole country lies at the feet of the emigrant, ready to be possessed. For the sum of 32s. you may travel in a few hours to Bathurst, the capital of the West.

11. All this may be enjoyed among a people whose whole social life is so like Home that it is scarcely possible for the emigrant to feel like "a stranger in a strange land." The language, customs, habits, laws, literature, education, religion, are all thoroughly English; life and property secure, and government free.

12. Every immigrant, if sober, healthy, and industrious, is wealth to the Colony, and is made welcome at once—never received with jealousy and suspicion. All that Australia wants to make her one of the wealthiest if not *the* wealthiest of lands, is population. Everything else she offers, and on the most generous terms. Farm labourers, miners, domestic servants, mechanics, and artisans of all sorts, enterprising capitalists of large means or small, if they are only temperate, able, and willing to work, may make sure of improving their condition by emigrating to New South Wales. In fact, it matters not what a man has been accustomed to in the Old World, if he is willing to throw away dilletanteism, take off his coat, turn up his sleeves, and put his shoulder to the wheel of fortune just as it may be presented to him—not the slave of false pride and miscalled respectability, but making the best of such opportunities as may come across his path—there is prosperity awaiting him on these shores, a certain competence, and not unlikely an ample fortune. Here children are a real blessing. The father's brow is never clouded with anxiety at every new addition to his family, wondering how the little mouth is to be filled; unless false notions of gentility have poisoned his colonial blood, and he is ashamed to let his children degrade themselves with business. If he be rich, he can afford to indulge that sublime luxury, but he would be a better citizen and patriot if he would dispense with it. We have land enough and to spare

for many generations; it will yield nearly everything that has any value in the markets of the World. Healthy labour is all we ask for; capital, too, where it is available, and that will smooth the lot of labour,—but healthy labour is the one great requisite, and whoever can offer us that is welcome. To all who are struggling to get on at Home and yet can hardly keep their heads above the water, and in their old age must depend upon their children or their parish, we say, gather together what little substance you have, bid farewell to your native land, come out to this Land of Plenty; and, under its brighter sky, let that same labour of yours, which at Home cannot save you from the fear of being a burden to your Country, win for you a fair day's wage for a fair day's work; and, an Englishman still, you need love your fatherland none the less, but help to preserve her Empire and augment her greatness through all future ages.

Sydney, February, 1873.

XX.—APPENDIX.

Gold Fields in New South Wales.

Southern District.

	sq. ms.		sq. ms.		sq. ms.
Burrangong	424	Muttuma	30	Shoalhaven	54
Black Creek	1	Long Flat	1	Jembaicumbene	5
Araluen	55	Moruya	8	Mongarlow	40
Narraga	2	Tumberumba	210	Kiandra	495
Delegate	100	Crackenbac	5	Gulph	9
Adelong Creek	120	Marragle	97	New Marraglo	5
Corowa	10	Gundagal	9	Adgimbilly	180
Black Range, at Albury	18	Emu Creek	312	Mogo	57
Nerrimunga	65	Nanima	95	Coobarra Gundia	256
Ouranee	46	Sharp's Creek	32	Gundaroo	84
Jugiong Creek	47				

Western District.

	sq. ms.		sq. ms.		sq. ms.
Kirkconnell	71	Bathurst	5	Macquarie River	18
Cheshire's Creek	15	Winburndale Rivulet	3	Turon	800
Cudgegong River	103	Grattal Creek	3	Stoney Creek and Iron-	
Muckrawa	25	Ophir	140	barks	32
Caloola Creek	22	Campbell's River	80	King's Plains	5
Tuena	15	Cook's Vale	15	Abercrombie	800
Rocky Bridge	21	Gilmandike	70	Isabella River	12
Lachlan	1,000	Mitchell's Creek	80	Pipeclay Creek	20
Billabong	409	Taglow Creek	15	Meroo	383
Tallawang	31	Wood's Flat	35	Cargo	35
Belabula	22½	Benereo	12	Gulgong	3,000
Gunner's Dam	1	Apple-tree Flat	63	Buckenbar	7½
Oberon	100			Chambers' Creek	57½

Northern District.

	sq. ms.		sq. ms.		sq. ms.
Peel River	70	Bingham	143	Rocky River	73
Tooloom Creek	66	Timbarra	1000	Ironbark	75
Upper Hunter	92	Boyd	84	Boorook, Lunatic	477
Cangal	69	Solferino	200		

The approximate total area of Gold Fields proclaimed, 13,656 square miles.

GOVERNOR.

SIR HERCULES GEORGE ROBERT ROBINSON, K.C.M.G.

MINISTRY.

Chief Secretary and Premier—The Honorable **HENRY PARKES.**
Treasurer and Secretary for Finance and Trade.} The Honorable **GEORGE ALFRED LLOYD.**
Secretary for Lands—The Honorable **JAMES SQUIRE FARNELL.**
Secretary for Public Works—The Honorable **JOHN SUTHERLAND.**
Attorney General—The Honorable **EDWARD BUTLER.**
Solicitor General—The Honorable **JOSEPH GEORGE LONG INNES.**
Postmaster General and Vice-President of the Executive Council.} The Honorable **SAUL SAMUEL.**

STATISTICS, 1851 TO 1871.

Year.	Population.	Births.	Marriages.	Deaths.	Schools.		Grants for Primary Education.
					Schools.	Number of Scholars.	
1851	197,168	7,675	1,915	2,600	423	21,120	
1852	208,254	7,866	2,175	3,605	351	23,668	
1853	231,088	8,860	2,569	4,176	420	25,660	
1854	251,315	9,063	2,761	4,511	413	25,953	
1855	277,579	10,344	2,765	4,022	476	27,243	
1856	286,873	10,097	2,778	4,203	565	29,426	
1857	305,487	12,501	2,902	4,846	550	29,236	£41,827
1858	342,062	13,802	2,992	5,883	653	33,236	41,617
1859	a336,572	14,415	3,295	5,642	739	32,840	41,605
1860	348,546	14,233	2,945	6,562	798	34,767	51,693
1861	358,278	14,681	3,222	5,343	849	37,874	51,872
1862	367,495	15,434	3,326	6,524	925	42,211	62,062
1863	378,934	15,679	3,314	6,653	976	46,810	71,734
1864	392,589	16,881	3,480	6,445	1,022	48,427	71,627
1865	411,388	17,283	3,578	6,596	1,069	53,453	71,657
1866	431,412	16,950	3,402	7,361	1,155	59,594	81,671
1867	447,620	18,317	3,426	8,631	1,180	63,183	79,594
1868	466,705	18,485	3,736	7,225	1,254	66,835	91,426
1869	485,356	19,243	3,799	6,691	1,304	71,523	106,282
1870	502,861	19,648	3,848	6,558	1,381	74,503	105,732
1871	519,182	20,143	3,953	6,407	1,450	77,889	111,601

a Queensland was separated from New South Wales, June 6, 1859.
£15,000 a-year are voted by Parliament for University, Libraries, Schools of Art, &c.
The amount of gold coined at Sydney Mint to 31st December, 1872, was £32,354,000.
The amount granted for primary education for 1872 was £132,000.

STATISTICS OF NEW SOUTH WALES—1851 TO 1871.

Year.	Land Sales. Quantity.	Land Sales. Amount realized.	Acres under crop.	Live Stock. Horses.	Live Stock. Horned Cattle.	Live Stock. Sheep.	Live Stock. Pigs.
	acres.	£					
1851	24,030	64,425	153,117¼	116,397	1,375,257	7,890,895	65,510
1852	26,550	55,808	131,730¼	123,404	1,495,984	7,707,917	78,550
1853	73,075	211,035	139,014½	139,765	1,552,285	7,929,708	71,395
1854	83,396	319,533	131,857	148,851	1,576,750	8,144,119	63,255
1855	127,952	270,630	171,100¼	158,159	1,858,407	8,602,490	68,091
1856	167,753	245,555	186,033½	168,920	2,023,418	7,730,323	105,908
1857	145,102	210,333	184,513¼	160,053	2,148,664	8,144,162	109,166
1858	169,214	240,633	223,295¼	200,713	2,110,604	7,581,762	92,843
1859	135,107	252,627	247,542⅜	214,684	2,190,976	5,162,071	119,701
1860	109,216	155,316	260,798	251,497	2,408,586	6,119,163	180,662
1861	189,930	222,594	297,575	233,220	2,271,923	5,015,954	146,091
1862	67,292 a357,250	216,088	302,183½	273,389	2,020,383	6,145,651	125,541
1863	92,016 a259,369	192,113	307,035	262,554	2,032,522	7,790,069	135,899
1864	58,216 a165,616	112,710	318,854	284,567	1,924,110	8,271,520	104,154
1865	101,350 a151,450	213,241	378,254½	282,587	1,961,905	8,132,511	146,901
1866	100,177 a358,652	261,590	451,225¼	278,437	1,771,809	11,562,155	137,915
1867	119,044 a232,176	204,060	413,164	280,201	1,728,427	13,909,574	173,168
1868	149,945 a239,516	265,250	434,756¼	280,818	1,701,411	15,080,625	176,901
1869	104,800 a397,328	319,613	482,324½	280,304	1,795,004	14,989,923	175,024
1870	94,373 a329,318	250,843	420,976	337,597	2,195,096	16,308,585	243,066
1871	88,637 a358,682	... ...	417,801	304,100	2,014,888	16,278,697	213,193

a Lands conditionally sold under the "Crown Lands Alienation Act of 1861."

Lands leased for mining purposes are: gold, 64,000 acres; coal, 34,720; tin, copper, lead, silver, and other minerals, 396,228 acres.

Crops grown are: Wheat, maize, barley, oats, hay, rye, millet, sorghum, sugar-cane, arrow-root, potatoes, tobacco, grapes, oranges, and most other fruits and vegetables.

Fruit exported, 1871 (mostly oranges), 146,751 pkgs.; value, £49,312.

Maize exported, 1871, 732,657 bushels and bags; value, £109,413.

Sugar produced to 1871—value, £150,000.

STATISTICS OF NEW SOUTH WALES—1851 TO 1871.

Year.	Mills.	Manufactories, Works, &c.	Coal Mines.		Shipping.				Value of total Imports.	Value of total Exports.
					Inwards.		Outwards.			
			Quantity.	Value.	Number of Vessels.	Tonnage.	Number of Vessels.	Tonnage.		
			tons.	£					£	£
1851	151	140	67,610	25,546	553	153,002	503	139,020	1,563,931	1,796,912
1852	145	141	67,404	36,885	721	197,366	701	175,960	1,900,436	4,604,034
1853	143	141	96,809	78,059	1,048	336,852	1,061	341,540	6,342,397	4,523,346
1854	140	146	116,642	119,380	1,058	376,927	1,112	409,489	5,981,063	4,050,126
1855	147	255	137,076	89,082	1,152	353,323	1,185	362,482	4,668,519	2,884,130
1856	154	314	189,960	117,906	1,143	321,679	1,219	336,113	5,460,971	3,430,880
1857	157	284	210,434	148,158	1,100	351,413	1,204	377,147	6,729,408	4,011,952
1858	169	295	216,397	162,162	1,141	348,984	1,254	366,825	6,059,366	4,186,277
1859	177	549	308,213	204,371	1,250	363,121	1,299	387,015	6,597,053	4,768,049
1860	193	745	368,862	226,493	1,424	427,835	1,438	431,484	7,519,285	5,072,020
1861	184	788	342,067	218,820	1,327	366,236	1,391	379,460	6,391,555	5,594,839
1862	181	859	476,522	305,234	1,493	454,837	1,568	467,356	9,334,645	7,102,562
1863	180	1,768	433,889	236,230	1,494	479,827	1,603	511,373	8,319,576	6,936,839
1864	174	2,084	549,012	270,171	1,849	607,168	1,842	647,057	10,135,708a	9,037,832a
1865	175	2,132	585,525	274,303	1,912	635,888	2,120	690,294	10,635,507a	9,563,818a
1866	159	2,389	774,238	324,049	2,099	730,354	2,259	784,381	9,403,192a	9,913,839a
1867	188	2,274	770,012	342,655	1,868	646,970	2,104	726,721	6,599,804	6,880,715
1868	181	3,562	954,231	417,809	2,073	724,193	2,218	776,449	8,051,377	7,192,904
1869	183	4,497	919,774	346,146	2,022	741,369	2,236	833,248	8,392,753a	9,933,442a
1870	187	6,862	868,564	316,836	1,858	689,820	2,066	771,942	7,757,281a	7,900,038a
1871	190	6,827	898,784	316,340	1,891	706,019	2,123	794,460	9,009,508a	11,245,032a

a Inclusive of the Traffic Overland.

Principal manufactures are: Iron works, flour, steam saw, sugar, bone, cloth and paper mills; leather, oil, and tobacco factories; ship-building (iron and wood), smelting and chemical works.

Tonnage of ships built in the Colony, 76,700, and of shipping now owned in the Colony, 75,224 tons.

Kerosene shale produced, 1871,—14,700 tons; stated value, £34,050.

Copper produced in 1871—668 tons; stated value, £47,275

Tin exported 1872:—Ingot 91 tons 18 cwt.; value, £12,623; ore, 1,031 tons 12 cwt.; value, £75,955. Total quantity received from the mines at Sydney in 1872, 1,730 tons 1 cwt.; value, £123,274.

Coal raised from New South Wales mines to end of 1871, was 9,816,633 tons, of which 5,885,493 tons valued at £3,790,223.

STATISTICS OF NEW SOUTH WALES—1851 TO 1871.

Year.	Telegrams.	Postal.			Money Orders.		Revenue (including Loans).	Expenditure (including Loans).
		Letters.	Newspapers.	Packets, &c.	Number.	Amount.		
						£	£	£
1851	....	975,318	762,487	....	....	....	436,698	444,108
1852	....	1,117,777	1,023,678	....	....	....	682,137	600,322
1853	....	1,587,407	1,515,580	....	....	....	987,477	682,621
1854	....	1,837,591	1,919,192	....	....	....	1,239,147	1,136,569
1855	....	2,114,179	2,100,989	....	....	....	1,660,710	1,675,024
1856	....	2,368,938	2,081,347	....	....	....	1,986,553	1,835,132
1857	....	2,602,919	2,214,411	....	....	....	1,531,137	1,543,328
1858	9,141	3,483,209	2,608,140	68,564	....	....	1,456,451	1,570,560
1859	36,807	3,977,820	3,168,299	70,945	....	....	2,339,490	1,858,166
1860	53,951	4,230,761	3,668,783	83,736	....	....	1,880,508	2,047,955
1861	74,204	4,369,463	3,384,245	105,338	....	....	1,843,067	1,973,229
1862	104,660	5,092,545	3,460,936	170,782	....	....	2,273,170	2,135,518
1863	124,638	5,662,839	4,554,739	276,814	11,478	53,861	2,199,163	2,602,094
1864	130,500	5,963,562	4,600,077	287,540	21,912	105,899	1,984,775	2,326,901
1865	138,785	6,329,353	4,689,858	249,904	28,469	130,747	2,237,234	2,314,794
1866	143,523	6,678,371	4,513,185	249,939	41,968	196,071	3,253,179	3,012,571
1867	130,447	6,748,356	3,897,905	189,297	60,846	240,062	2,569,456	2,935,633
1868	132,872	6,555,890	3,580,332	116,987	56,492	247,488	4,093,812	3,286,839
1869	145,370	7,143,638	3,593,553	158,034	66,062	288,476	3,663,509	3,265,805
1870	173,812	7,083,500	3,814,700	157,700	65,743	289,325	2,575,309	3,298,353
1871	218,530	7,509,500	3,992,100	158,300	69,750	293,370	4,709,010	4,179,840

Money deposited in the Banks, 1872.—£10,411,160.

Railways:—Cost, £6,653,413; miles opened, 396½; extensions projected, 283 miles.

Telegraphs:—cost, £212,255; miles opened in 1872, 6,114.

Roads:—10,000 miles; number of miles travelled by postal conveyances, 1872,—3,252,888.

Public works:—Amount voted by Parliament out of current revenue for, in 1872,—£642,856.

STATISTICS OF NEW SOUTH WALES—1851 TO 1871.

	Exports, the Produce of the Colony.							
Year.	Wool.		Hides & Leather	Tallow.	Gold.*		Coal.	Timber.
	Quantity.	Value.	Value.	Value.	Quantity.	Value.	Quantity. Value.	Value.
	lbs.	£	£	£		£	tons £	£
1851	15,269,317	828,342	....	114,168	144,120	468,336	28,470 12,027	17,462
1852	11,086,974	676,815	....	146,811	818,751	2,660,946	24,794 100,951	17,330
1853	16,358,869	999,896	41,159	154,703	548,052	1,781,172	51,501 81,078	32,217
1854	18,976,300	1,181,956	44,936	164,256	237,910	773,209	59,297 101,752	62,365
1855	17,671,684	1,078,017	42,782	123,255	64,384	209,250	61,484 58,893	44,777
1856	19,200,341	1,303,070	64,638	137,202	42,463	138,007	84,086 65,739	42,333
1857	17,044,201	1,275,067	122,653	82,134	253,564	983,850	96,457 45,960	48,734
1858	13,553,835	1,126,486	61,844	53,186	254,907	994,960	113,649 89,200	36,645
1859	16,988,016	1,458,005	98,542	37,275	435,996	1,696,078	173,935 132,984	47,154
1860	12,809,362	1,123,699	90,554	28,794	483,012	1,876,049	233,877 183,761	28,186
1861	12,745,891	1,396,420	100,459	60,816	488,293	1,890,908	207,780 160,965	19,554
1862	13,482,139	1,283,818	105,456	104,030	699,566	2,715,037	308,782 245,422	25,318
1863	14,791,849	1,262,274	119,004	81,221	605,722	2,361,949	298,038 220,181	42,190
1864	25,827,917a	2,294,615a	129,122	100,654	758,109	2,952,471	372,466 212,483	37,772
1865	29,858,791a	2,283,500a	98,110	122,270	662,521	2,647,668	382,968 214,158	36,105
1866	36,980,685a	2,830,348a	113,045	51,626	751,700	2,924,891	540,905 300,588	25,315
1867	21,708,902	1,711,322	105,487	63,648	660,619	2,586,044	473,357 253,259	17,541
1868	25,721,032	1,879,751	105,995	144,377	487,600	1,896,929	548,036 292,201	12,707
1869	51,209,672a	3,762,522a	113,922	167,536	641,069	2,480,145	595,553 298,195	23,159
1870	47,440,610a	2,741,141a	120,971	223,787	410,547	1,585,736	578,389 267,651	22,037
1871	65,611,953a	4,748,160a	177,262	245,727	535,492	2,074,937	565,429 256,690	28,455

a Includes traffic overland.
* Includes gold from other Colonies minted at Sydney.

Value of gold, exported from New South Wales, to 31st December, 1872,—£40,095,823.
Approximate area of proclaimed Gold Fields, 13,656 square miles.

Preserved and salted meat exported in 1871, the produce of the Colony, was valued at £133,266.

Value of pastoral exports, 1871,—£3,598,623.

Total pastoral exports, seaward, from New South Wales, to 31st December, 1871,—Wool, 733,248,693 lbs., value, £50,388,813; tallow, 2,130,175 cwt., value, £3,365,589. Value of oil exported, £2,501,660.

NEW SOUTH WALES:

THE OLDEST AND RICHEST OF THE AUSTRALIAN COLONIES.

EXTRACTS FROM THE NEWSPAPERS.

From Speech of His Excellency SIR HERCULES ROBINSON, *at Bathurst, 6 March,* 1873.

I know of no sight more calculated to impress an Englishman with feelings of pride and thankfulness than to travel through a great new Country like this, and to see on all sides the evidence which it affords of industrial progress and social improvement,—to see scattered everywhere thriving bustling townships and homesteads, where, but a few years since, there was only the wigwam of the savage,— to see lands, which, within the memory of the present generation, were unproductive swamps and primeval forests, covered with flocks and herds and corn, and administering to the wants and contributing to the happiness of hundreds of thousands of the human race,—and above all to see the land inhabited by thriving communities of citizens, who are striving to attain a high moral standard, who are enjoying to the utmost degree constitutional liberty, and who are proving by their loyalty and good order how well they appreciate its blessings. I say that a sight such as this always makes me feel proud of the genius of my countrymen for colonization, and justifies me in looking forward with confidence to the future of this great Country. The resources of the land are boundless, and thousands upon thousands of working men who are often suffering in the Old Country from want or insufficient means would here find an easy and comfortable subsistence.

From Speech of His Excellency SIR HERCULES ROBINSON, *at Orange,* 10 *March,* 1873.

I can assure you that I have enjoyed my visit intensely to this beautiful and interesting district, which possesses such an unrivalled climate, and which is so rich in mineral and agricultural resources. It was at Ophir, in this neighbourhood, about twenty years ago, that gold was first discovered in Australia. Since then, silver, copper, lead, tin, and iron have all been found in this district, and there are abundant indications that this neighbourhood is as rich in mineral wealth as any part of the Colony. The land about Orange is capable of growing as fine wheat crops as any in the World; and I am glad to learn that the average produce per acre of the harvest which has been just reaped is over 25 bushels, whilst in some instances the yield has reached 35 and 40 bushels per acre. The district produces also fine crops of oats, barley, maize, pease, vetches, potatoes, and beet-root, whilst the show of all descriptions of English fruit and vegetables, which I have myself seen in the gardens of the neighbourhood, could not be surpassed by the produce of the richest market gardens in the Old Country. As far as it is possible to forecast the future, there appear to be years of great prosperity in store for New South Wales. The policy which is being pursued by the Government is, I venture to pronounce, a wise and far-seeing one. It is their desire to free industry, to facilitate and cheapen the means of communication, to offer easy terms for the acquisition of land, and to frame regulations for the encouragement and the development of the marvellous mineral resources of the Country. The Colony also possesses many great and remarkable natural advantages. Its central position, vast area, rich resources, magnificent harbour, with coal and iron close to navigable waters, all point it out as the first of Australian Colonies, and eventually as the head-quarters of Australian Confederation.

From Speech of His Excellency SIR HERCULES ROBINSON, *at Hill End,* 13 *March,* 1873.

Ever since my arrival in New South Wales I have heard of the marvellous wealth of your golden mountain, and have felt a strong desire to inspect the place for myself; but I may say that the picture which my fancy had painted fell far short of the reality which I have witnessed since my arrival here. I had seen a photograph of your main street, taken about eighteen months ago, with a bullock team dragging a waggon out of a swamp opposite the door of this hotel. I had heard also that, a couple of years ago, the place consisted only of a few hovels; and judging too, by the condition of the approach, I certainly did not expect to find much of a settlement at the end of it. But to my surprise, I found a large well laid out town, with straight streets and well built stores and business premises, four churches and parsonages, three banks, two newspapers, a public school, and a hospital; and in short, an appearance on all sides of comfort and stability and importance which would have been creditable in a city of fifty years' standing. As regards the population, I thought that perhaps I might have been met by a few hundreds of rough but enthusiastic miners; but to my astonishment, I was received at the entrance to the town by about three thousand well-dressed, orderly, and intelligent-looking men and women, accompanied by five hundred of as beautiful children as ever I saw in my life, and the whole procession headed by the members of the various Societies of Freemasons, Oddfellows, and Temperance Unions; whilst the whole body appeared to me to be animated by a feeling of enthusiastic loyalty which convinced me that, although oceans separate you from the Old Country, your hearts are British still, and that you retain in your distant isolated mountain home of Tambaroora those feelings of personal devotion to the Queen, respect for constituted authority, and love of law and order, which form the marked characteristics of the Anglo-Saxon race. Having had an opportunity of inspecting to-day most of your principal mines, I must say that it gave me great pleasure to find that they were all being worked in an honest, open, and straightforward manner, in the interest of their shareholders, and not with any reference to the manœuvres of the bulls and the bears of the Sydney Stock Exchange. I was much amused a few weeks since, in Sydney, to hear one morning that the city was much depressed, as Krohmann's had only declared a dividend of 12s. 6d. Now, considering that this dividend was 62½ per cent. upon the original capital, and considering also that the mine had yielded a few months before 20s. 6d., making a total cash return in about nine months of 165 per cent. on the capital, I confess I could not see any great cause for depression.

From Speech of Hon. J. G. Francis, Chief Secretary and Premier of Victoria.
Lithgow Valley, 25*th January,* 1873.

The present company are met to inspect and admire one of the grandest feats which civilization has accomplished. I will not limit my expression to "south of the line," in speaking of a public work in which so much enterprise, professional skill and public spirit, have been crowned with success. The initiation of such a work as this must have seemed impossible to all but the greatest adepts in skill and science; and, to the Colony of New South Wales, that has had the pluck, the courage, and the means to encourage such science,—honor is due. The work is not only great, but it is unmistakeably grand to see Nature in its magnificence so subdued and utilized. I do not hesitate to say that until now I had no adequate idea of the grandeur of your public works, and I admit that every time I visit Port Jackson I have a growing wish that I could tow it away to Port Phillip.

From Speech of Sir Henry Ayers, Chief Secretary and Premier of South Australia.
Lithgow Valley, 25*th January,* 1873.

Like Mr. Francis, I have had some experience of the kindness and hospitality of the inhabitants of New South Wales, for like him I have had an opportunity of visiting this Colony once before, and I left it on that occasion with the impression that it was a most beautiful place, and that its people were kind and hospitable to a degree. Twelve years have passed away since then. I have in the interval had an opportunity of visiting Europe and seeing a considerable part of the World, and I return to find that my admiration of New South Wales was not equal to that which it deserves, and to find that the people are quite as kind and hospitable now as they were then. I have spent upwards of thirty-three years of my life in South Australia, and I am wedded to it by ties of great interest, and I will say patriotism. If, however, I were not a South Australian, I should like to be a New South Welshman.

From Speech of the Hon. F. M. Innes, Treasurer and Premier of Tasmania. Sydney, February, 1873.

I did not require to tread upon these shores the other day for the first time to learn what the institutions of the Colony are, or what is the provision made by the Legislature for education and benevolent purposes in New South Wales. I did not require to be carried rapidly the other day along the railway, and to be brought face to face with Nature in some of its wildest forms, and to recognize there the mastery of your energy, enterprise, and resource. I knew what you had accomplished; but still I say that, for the complete success of the political institutions which have been transplanted to these new lands, we must look to the discipline of the people and the experience of the future. No one who has cast even a glance over this Colony, as I have been able to do, can doubt that great prosperity awaits this land, not only from the magnitude of its material resources, but from that spirit of enterprise which sees no difficulties, which so largely animates its people.

From Speech of Hon. E. Langton, Treasurer, Victoria. Sydney, 6 February, 1873.

Many years before I came to this part of the World, I read charming descriptions of the scenery in the neighbourhood of Sydney. Having seen it, I have no hesitation in saying that I believe there is no spot on this planet so beautiful. I rejoice with you in the beauty of your landscapes, and in the great commercial advantages which you possess.

From Speech of Hon. W. H. Reynolds, Commissioner of Trade and Customs, New Zealand. Sydney, 6 February, 1873.

The population of New Zealand is comparatively small, but before five years it will exceed that of Victoria. I will not say that it will exceed that of New South Wales, because I have very great faith in the prosperity of this Colony, and I believe that New South Wales and Queensland will take the lead in the Australian Group, and that New Zealand will rank third.

From Speech of the Hon. J. M. Thompson, Minister for Lands, Queensland. 15 February, 1873.

I shall always entertain a loyal feeling towards this Country, in which I was born; and I am more than pleased with the evidences of prosperity I see on every hand in this Colony of New South Wales. Not only are fortunes made, but, as the Premier of New Zealand has said, the people themselves appear to be in such prosperous circumstances, that the problem of the day will soon be what to do with the accumulation of riches.

From Speech of the Hon. Henry Parkes, Chief Secretary and Premier of New South Wales. 15 February, 1873.

We entertain an ardent desire that only one feeling should prevail in these great communities, and that is, a feeling of attachment to the Parent State, and a friendly desire to assist each other in the race of progress. It has been said by one of those voices which influence the progress of great communities, that " emulation has a thousand sons"; and I rejoice to see that, in this hemisphere, emulation has at least seven daughters. I rejoice in the free, vigorous, bold spirit of emulation which exists amongst these free communities springing from the Parent State. I trust that this legitimate emulation will never be narrowed by any unworthy feeling; that while we strive side by side, each doing his best to carve for himself the highest mark in the race of progress, we shall still remember that we are children of the same Parent State, that we inherit the same glories of that great Country which has been the pioneer of freedom all over the World, and that our destiny is one of common importance and distinction. The people of New South Wales have no cause to envy the progress of any one of the Colonies. We feel conscious that we have within our own bounds all the elements of national greatness; and while we wish them God-speed in their respective courses of progress, we feel at liberty to tell them that we shall endeavour yet to assert our position as the leader of them all. We feel that our resources justify the hopes we entertain, that the resources of our intellect, our settled population, our accumulated wealth, and our public spirit, will enable us to accomplish all to which we aspire.

From the "Maryborough Advertiser," March, 1873.

When Mr. Parkes, at the picnic which he gave to the Members of the Intercolonial Conference during their stay in Sydney, declared that the Colony of New South Wales intended to resume and maintain the lead among her sisters, he seems to have "spoken by the card." He has a scheme of policy already prepared which, if he can only obtain the concurrence of the Legislature in its adoption, will undoubtedly enable the neighbouring Colony to secure that pre-eminence which she is so anxious to obtain. A telegram from Sydney, which was published on Monday last, announces that the first business of the ensuing Session of the New South Wales Parliament will be the introduction of a Bill to revise the tariff, including the entire abolition of the ad valorem duties. Capital and enterprise naturally gravitate towards those Countries in which there is cheap coal, cheap iron, cheap living, and cheap raw material. If our neighbours in New South Wales establish free trade, and are content to raise their Customs revenue as Great Britain does, from about a dozen articles, such as tea, sugar, coffee, brandy, wine, and tobacco, Sydney will be the cheapest place in Australia to live. Cheap living implies a cheap labour; and with cheap labour, in addition to abundance of coal and iron, and a noble harbour, splendid docks, and a railway system facilitating the distribution of commodities to all parts of the Colony, the capital of New South Wales may not improperly aspire to take the lead both in manufactures and commerce.

When Mr. Parkes spoke of the future of New South Wales (observes " Ægles," in the *Australasian* of March 24, 1873), and of her outstripping Victoria in material prosperity, he was not so far out of his reckoning as some unthinking people imagined. New South Wales has a greater extent of territory, is richer in minerals generally, has longer and cheaper railways, and possesses magnificent coal measures. Isn't there significance in the fact that the debentures of New South Wales, which were far below those of Victoria in market value, now stand level with ours? Without a Victorian coal field, I will back Mr. Parkes in his forecast of our being ultimately passed in the race by New South Wales. We claim for Melbourne the honor of being the terminus of a mail line, and we haven't a pound of Victorian coal to sell to the steamers.

From the "Sydney Morning Herald."

On Thursday, 20th March, 1873, His Excellency the Governor and Lady Robinson, accompanied by the Colonial Secretary (the Honorable Henry Parkes), visited Mr. F. L. Edwards's store, to inspect the splendid specimens from Krohmann's mine which he is about to take to England. These specimens, numbering some half a dozen, weigh about 56 lbs., and appear to contain more gold than quartz. They are not merely flecked with the precious metal, but have threads of it of various thicknesses running right through. One lump has on its side a small piece cracked all round in such a way as to induce the belief that it could be easily separated from the larger mass. We saw an attempt of this kind made, yet such was the strength of its golden attachments that it could not be moved. Mr. Edwards, who leaves by the mail steamer on Tuesday, intends exhibiting them at the London Exhibition and elsewhere, in order to convince our English friends that the reputation which Hawkins Hill has obtained is based on something more than mere rumour. They are magnificent proofs that New South Wales contains the richest gold mines in the World; and, if a prize is offered for specimens of auriferous quartz, the judges will have little difficulty in making their award.

ADVERTISEMENTS.

VICTORIA INSURANCE COMPANIES.

FIRE AND MARINE, LIFE AND GUARANTEE.
United Capital ... ... £2,200,000.
Established, 1849.

Local Directors:
George Thorne, Esq., | J. de V. Lamb, Esq.

Fire Department: The premiums are the lowest that can be accepted with safety to the Insured and the Company.

Marine Risks at lowest current rates.

Fidelity Guarantee Policies issued at lowest current rates, with periodical reductions, to Government and Bank Officials and others holding situations of trust.

Private Sureties can obtain Indemnity Policies from this Company, securing themselves against loss arising through the dishonesty of the person for whom they have become surety.

Life Assurance, Endowment, or Annuity Policies granted at low rates of premium.

Life Assurance combined with **Guarantee** secures important reductions in the premium.

Forms of Proposal and full particulars upon application to any of the Agents, or to the Resident Secretary.

New South Wales Branch: New Pitt-street, Sydney.

FREDK. J. JACKSON, Resident Secretary.

AGENTS WANTED.

The above Companies are prepared to appoint Private and Public Agents in Country Districts where no such appointments have yet been made. Applications to be addressed to the Resident Secretary.

VICTORIA LIFE AND GENERAL INSURANCE COMPANY.

NEW PITT-STREET, SYDNEY.

Life Insurances effected on most favourable terms, and when combined with fidelity guarantees, at very reduced rates.

Fidelity Guarantee Policies issued to all Departments of the Government Service.

FREDK. J. JACKSON, Resident Secretary.

COLONIAL SUGAR REFINING COMPANY.

Established 1855, for the Manufacture of Raw and Refined Sugars, and the Distillation of Spirits, &c.

OFFICES: 24, BRIDGE-STREET, SYDNEY, N.S.W.

Directors:—Edward Knox, Esq., Chairman; Thomas Buckland, Esq. (Messrs. D. Cooper & Co.); Fred. C. Griffiths, Esq. (Messrs. Fanning, Griffiths, & Co.); Walter Lamb, Esq. J.P.; Alfred Stanger Leathes, Esq. (Liverpool, London, and Globe Insurance Company.)

General Manager:—J. Grafton Ross.

SUGAR MILLS.

Edward William Knox, Inspector.

Name of Mill.	Capacity per Season.	Locality.	Manager.
Chatsworth	2,500 tons Sugar	Clarence River	W. A. Poolman
Harwood	2,500 do.	Do.	C. W. Stephens
Southgate	2,000 do.	Do.	E. W. S. Hayley.

SUGAR REFINERY:
Parramatta-street, Sydney.

DISTILLERIES:
Parramatta-street, Sydney.
Harwood Island, Clarence River.

AGENTS IN LONDON:
Messrs. F. Parbury & Co., 7, East India Avenue.

BANKERS:
Oriental Bank Corporation.

BULLI COAL-MINING COMPANY.
(Incorporated, 1862.)

Capital, £37,000; Amount paid up, £36,465.

Directors:—G. Wigram Allen, Esq., M.L.A., Chairman; The Honorable George Allen, Esq., M.L.C.; A. H. C. Macafee, Esq.; Edwin T. Beilby, Esq.; and R. G. Reading, Esq.

Manager:—James Shoobert.

Offices:—1 and 3, Exchange, Sydney, N.S.W.

APART from their extensive local and intercolonial trade, this Company executes orders for delivery of Coal at San Francisco, Java, Mauritius, or any of the Ports of India and China; and having a line of their own screw steam Colliers running from their Mines at Bulli, N.S.W. (about 40 miles south of the Port of Sydney), can ensure the loading of vessels with great despatch.

COPY of Report (dated March 23rd, 1872), of Royal School of Mines, London, on Bulli Coal.

I herewith forward the result of the examination of the Bulli Coal from New South Wales:—

COMPOSITION.	PER CENT.
Carbon	75·57
Hydrogen	4·70
Oxygen and Nitrogen	4·99
Sulphur	0·54
Ash	13·17
Water	1·03
	100·00

The colour of the ash is reddish white.

Specific gravity .... 1·471

When the portion of the powdered Coal is heated in a closed vessel, the gases evolved burn with a yellow luminous somewhat smoky flame, and a slightly lustrous coherent Coke is left, which differs little in bulk from the original Coal.

The percentage results obtained are as follows:—

Coke	74·78
Volatile Gaseous matters	24·19
Water	1·03
	100·00

The theoretical calorific or evaporative power, that is, the weight of water converted into steam by 1 lb. of the Coal, as determined by experiment with the calorimeter, is 12·21 lbs. A second experiment gave a like result.

The actual evaporative power of a fuel as found in practice differs from the theoretical, and varies with the construction of the furnace, form of boiler, mode of burning, and other obvious circumstances.

I am, gentlemen,
for DR. PERCY,
Yours faithfully,
RICHARD SMITH.

ADVERTISEMENTS.

ALDERSON & SONS,

TANNERS, CURRIERS,

Enamelled and Japanned Leather Dressers,

AND

MANUFACTURERS

OF ALL DESCRIPTIONS OF

Saddlery, Harness, Mill-Bands,

MEN'S WOMEN'S AND CHILDREN'S

PEGGED AND RIVETED BOOTS

AND

BOOT UPPERS:

MERCHANTS & IMPORTERS

OF

SADDLERS' IRONMONGERY, GRINDERY & ELASTIC WEBBING

AND

ALL KINDS OF FANCY LEATHERS.

WHOLESALE WAREHOUSE:
221, ELIZABETH STREET, SYDNEY.

TANNERY & MANUFACTORY:
BOURKE STREET, SURRY HILLS.

FELLMONGERY ESTABLISHMENT:
WATERLOO.

AUSTRALIAN BREADSTUFFS.

The undersigned are desirous of notifying to Grain Merchants and Flour Factors in the United Kingdom and elsewhere, that they devote special attention to, and have the largest Commission business in this Colony in the sale and purchase of Wheat and Flour.

Sydney is the chief depôt in the Australasian Colonies for the surplus productions of Wheat and Flour in the surrounding Colonies of South Australia, Victoria, Tasmania, and New Zealand; and the undersigned are Agents for most of the leading Millers and Shippers engaged in this trade at the principal ports, and are in receipt of continuous supplies. They have the experience of many years in executing Foreign Commissions, and, in their capacity of Agents, charter and load vessels direct from any of the grain-producing Colonies, or forward any quantities desired by the regular lines of ships trading to London and elsewhere.

No charge is made for chartering vessels or engaging freight. The usual Mercantile Commission of $2\frac{1}{2}$ per cent. covers execution of orders accompanied by Letters of Credit. Drafts under which at sixty days sight against shipping documents can be negotiated at from par to 1 per cent. premium. Insurances (free of particular average) range from 25s. to 30s. per cent., according to ports of loading and discharge.

WHEAT

Is shipped in the usual Dundee sacks, containing about $4\frac{1}{4}$ bushels.
Cost of sacks extra.

FLOUR

Is shipped in same kind of sacks of 200 lbs. net.
Cost of sacks included in price.

The superior quality of Australian Grain and Flour is now so universally known and understood in the United Kingdom, India, China, the Cape, Mauritius, Port de France, and many other parts of the world, that any further description is unnecessary.

Bankers:—Oriental Bank Corporation, and we should consequently prefer their Credits or references.

Agents in London:—Messrs. Johnson and Archer, No. 2, Lawrence Pountney Hill, Cannon-street.

EDWIN THOMAS BEILBY,
WALTER SCOTT,

Trading as—
BEILBY & SCOTT,
General Commission Merchants and Agents,
123, Pitt-street, Sydney.

AUSTRALIAN MERCANTILE & SHIPPING AGENCY.

The undersigned tender their Services for any matters pertaining to a General Commission Agency Business to which they devote their Special Attention, and can offer their constituents the advantage of over thirty years Commercial experience in this City.

EDWIN THOMAS BEILBY, } BEILBY & SCOTT.
WALTER SCOTT,

123, Pitt-street, North, Sydney.

Bankers:—Oriental Bank Corporation.
London Agents:—Johnson & Archer,
No. 2, Laurence, Pountney Hill, Cannon-street.

GRETA COAL AND SHALE MINE.

PORT OF NEWCASTLE, NEW SOUTH WALES.

The undersigned invite the special attention of Foreign Gas Companies and Steam Proprietors to the produce of this Mine being of the highest quality for *Gas, Steaming,* and *Household purposes,* and is shipped from Newcastle at a small advance on the price of the ordinary Shipping Coal.

Direct orders for Charters and Cargoes are executed by the undersigned free of Commission, the Mine being their own property.

123, Pitt-street, Sydney.　　　　　　　　　　　　BEILBY & SCOTT.

EDWIN THOMAS BEILBY, WALTER SCOTT, AND EDWARD ROW,

Trading under the firm and style of

EDWARD ROW & COMPANY,

Wholesale Importing Chemists and Druggists.
Exporters of Crude Minerals and Chemicals.
Contractors to the Government of New South Wales.
Agents for the Principal Patent Medicines and Medicinal Manufacturers of Europe and America.

219, PITT-STREET, SYDNEY.

COMMERCIAL BANKING COMPANY OF SYDNEY.

(*Incorporated by Act of Council,* 1848.)

CAPITAL, £400,000. RESERVE FUND, £170,000.

Directors:—Richard Jones, Esq., Chairman; Walter Lamb, Esq., Deputy Chairman; Edward Knox, Esq.; John Brewster, Esq.; F. H. Dangar, Esq.; T. A. Dibbs, Esq., Manager.
Auditors:—Charles Smith, Esq., and E. M. Stephen, Esq.
Solicitors:—Messrs. Want and Johnson.

Head Office—George-street, Sydney. T. A. Dibbs, Manager; F. N. Burt, Acting Manager; T. B. Gaden, Branch Inspector—with Branches at Haymarket, George-street South; and South Head Road.
London Office—39, Lombard-street, E.C. Directors:—J. A. Youl, Esq.; H. G. Smith, Esq.; and Charles Parbury, Esq. Manager:—Nathaniel Cork.
Branches in New South Wales:—Albury, Armidale, Bathurst, Bega, Berrima, Bombala, Bourke, Burrangong, Carcoar, Casino, Cooma, Dubbo, Goulburn, Hill End, Inverell, Kempsey, Kiama, Maitland, Milton, Morpeth, Murrurundi, Muswellbrook, Narrabri, Newcastle, Orange, Parramatta, Queanbeyan, Shoalhaven, Singleton, Tambaroora, Tamworth, Wollongong, Yass. And at Brisbane:—Bundaberg, Dalby, Gayndah, Maryborough, and Mackay, in Queensland. With the following

AGENCIES IN THE COLONIES:—

VICTORIA:—The Bank of Victoria, National Bank of Australasia, and Colonial Bank of Australasia. SOUTH AUSTRALIA:—The Bank of South Australia, the National Bank of Australasia, and the Bank of Adelaide. WEST AUSTRALIA:—National Bank of Australasia. TASMANIA:—The Bank of Van Diemen's Land. NEW ZEALAND:—The Bank of New Zealand.

IN GREAT BRITAIN, &c.:—

LONDON:—The London and Westminster Bank, and the London and County Bank. LIVERPOOL:—The Liverpool Union Bank. MANCHESTER:—The Manchester and Salford Bank. IRELAND:—The Belfast Banking Company, and the National Bank. SCOTLAND:—The Commercial Bank of Scotland. SAN FRANCISCO:—Messrs. Macoudray & Co., and the Bank of British Columbia. VALPARAISO:—Banco Nacional de Chile. NEW YORK:—Messrs. Drexel, Morgan, & Co. INDIA, CHINA, CEYLON, AND SINGAPORE:—The Chartered Mercantile Bank of India, London, and China. HONOLULU:—Messrs. Bishop & Co.

The Bank discount bills, grant cash credits, make advances on approved security, allow interest upon fixed deposits, issue drafts or letters of credit, and negotiate or collect bills payable at any of the above-named places or elsewhere, at current rates; collect dividends on shares in public Companies, and interest on debentures; act for their customers in the investment of money in securities in Great Britain or in the Colonies; and are prepared to undertake the agency of Banks on such terms as may be mutually agreed upon.

ADVERTISEMENTS.

THE AUSTRALIAN JOINT STOCK BANK.
(Incorporated by Act of Council, 1853.).

PAID-UP CAPITAL, £484,656, with power to increase to £1,000,000.

Directors :—J. S. Mitchell, Esq., Chairman ; William Moffitt, Esq.; Edward Lord, Esq.; John Frazer, Esq.; Robert Saddington, Esq.; Alexander Learmonth, Esq.
   Auditors :—T. B. Rolin, Esq.; J. G. Raphael, Esq.
   Solicitors :—Messrs. M'Carthy and Robertson.

HEAD OFFICE, SYDNEY.
Vincent Wanostrocht Giblin, General Manager. Edward Griffiths, Accountant.

LONDON OFFICE.
Directors:—James Henderson, Esq.; Paul Frederick Morgan, Esq.; William Mort, Esq. John Christie, Manager.

BRANCHES.
BRANCHES IN NEW SOUTH WALES.
Francis Adams, Branch Inspector.

Albury, Armidale, Bathurst, Braidwood, Currajong, Deniliquin, Forbes, Gulgong, Goulburn, Grafton, Grenfell, Hay, Hill End, Mudgee, Newcastle, Singleton, Solferino, Tambaroora, Taree, Tenterfield, Wagga Wagga, Wentworth, West Maitland, Yass.

BRANCHES IN QUEENSLAND.
H. P. Abbott, Branch Inspector.

Brisbane, Bowen, Clermont, Copperfield, Gladstone, Gympie, Ipswich, Mackay, Maryborough, Milchester, (Charters Towers), Ravenswood, Rockhampton, Stanthorpe, Toowoomba, Townsville, Warwick.

The Agents for the Bank in the Colonies are :—
For Victoria.....................	The Bank of Victoria.
,,	The English, Scottish, and Australian Chartered Bank.
,,	The National Bank of Australasia.
For Tasmania	The Bank of Van Diemen's Land.
For South Australia	The Bank of South Australia.
,,	The National Bank of Australasia.
For New Zealand	The Bank of New Zealand.
,,	The Bank of Otago (Limited), Dunedin.

FOR GREAT BRITAIN AND IRELAND:—
London—The Australian Joint Stock Bank, 18, King William-street, E.C.
London Bankers, and Agents for England generally—The National Provincial Bank of England.
Edinburgh and Scotland generally—The Royal Bank of Scotland.
Dublin and Ireland generally—The Provincial Bank of Ireland.
FOR NEW YORK AND THE UNITED STATES OF AMERICA :—
Messrs. Brown, Brothers and Co.
FOR SAN FRANCISCO :—
Agency of the Bank of British North America.

The Bank grants drafts and credits on all its Agents and Branches at current rates ; negotiates produce bills with documents ; discounts commercial paper ; collects dividends on local stock for its customers, free of commission ; and is open to transact every kind of banking business and agency.

ADVERTISEMENTS.

THE CITY BANK, SYDNEY.

PAID-UP CAPITAL, £240,000, with power to increase to £500,000.

DIRECTORS:—S. A. Joseph, Esq., Chairman; M. Alexander, Esq.; W. Forster, Esq., M.L.A.; John Alger, Esq.; James Watson, Esq., M.L.C.
AUDITORS:—E. Wrench, Esq.; Hon. John Blaxland, Esq., M.L.C.
MANAGER:—William Neill. SECRETARY:—Edmund Rouse.
ACCOUNTANT:—William Woolley. SOLICITOR:—W. W. Billyard, Esq.

Agents:—

London—The London Joint Stock Bank.
Scotland—The Commercial Bank of Scotland.
San Francisco—The Bank of California.
New York—Messrs. Lees and Waller, Bankers.
Hongkong—The Chartered Mercantile Bank of India, London and China.
Queensland—The Queensland National Bank.

Victoria—The National Bank of Australasia.
South Australia—Ditto ditto.
Western Australia—Ditto ditto.
Tasmania—The Bank of Van Diemen's Land.
New Zealand—The Bank of New Zealand.
New Caledonia—Compagnie de la Nouvelle Calédonie.

This Bank adopts and transacts all usual banking business with either of the places above mentioned.

The following Publications may be obtained at the Government Printing Office, Sydney.

THE INDUSTRIAL PROGRESS OF NEW SOUTH WALES,

CONTAINING A COLOURED MAP OF THE COLONY,

Showing the localities of the various Mining, Agricultural, and Pastoral Industries; the Gold Fields, Vine-growing Districts, and Coal Deposits, &c.

This Work embraces a general view of the progress of the Colony, during its first centenary period, in Arts, Manufactures, Agricultural, Pastoral, and Mineral pursuits; together with a Report of the Intercolonial Exhibition held at Sydney in the year 1870, and a Catalogue of the Exhibits, and Judges' Awards, as well as separate and Original Papers on the Sedimentary Formations of New South Wales, Mineralogy, Indigenous Woods, Orange Cultivation, Natural History, and other equally interesting subjects. The Book contains nearly 800 pages, royal 8vo. Price, in boards, 5s.; cloth, 10s.

THE PUBLIC STATUTES OF NEW SOUTH WALES,

From 7 Geo. IV to 25 Victoria. In 4 vols., cloth bound. Price £3. The subsequent Acts, from 26 to 34-5 Victoria inclusive, collected, quarter-bound, and lettered on edge to distinguish Sessional Parts. Price £2 6s.

The New South Wales Parliamentary Hand-book. Price 2s. 6d.

Crown Lands Acts of 1861, and Regulations thereunder (Eighth Edition). Price 1s. 6d.

The Gold Fields Act of 1866, and Regulations of 24th September, 1869, to 25th August, 1871, inclusive. Price, 1s.

THE MAMMALS OF AUSTRALIA,

Illustrated by MISS HARRIETT SCOTT and MRS. HELENA FORDE, for the Council of Education. With a short account of all the Species hitherto described, by GERARD KREFFT, F.L.S., Curator and Secretary of the Australian Museum. Price, 12s. 6d.

KREFFT'S SNAKES OF AUSTRALIA:

A descriptive Catalogue of all the known species, with a full account of their habits and geographical distribution; including hints with regard to the treatment of wounds inflicted by venomous Snakes. Illustrated by 12 Plates, on which all the known species are represented. Plain, 15s.; Coloured, 30s. To be had of all Booksellers.

THE FOSSIL FAUNA OF AUSTRALIA,

By GERARD KREFFT, F.L.S., with 18 Plates of Illustrations, by MISS HARRIETT SCOTT and MRS. HELENA FORDE.

THOMAS RICHARDS, Government Printer.

AUSTRALIAN MUTUAL PROVIDENT SOCIETY,

ESTABLISHED 1849,

FOR LIFE ASSURANCE ON THE MUTUAL PRINCIPLE.

PRINCIPAL OFFICE: 98, NEW PITT-STREET, SYDNEY.

Board of Directors:—George King, Esq., Chairman; Professor John Smith, M.D., Deputy Chairman; Samuel Lyons, Esq.; Edwin Thos. Beilby, Esq.; J. H. Goodlet, Esq.; John Fairfax, Esq.

Actuary:—Morrice A. Black, Esq., F.I.A.

Chief Medical Officer:—Sprott Boyd, Esq., M.D., 6, Lyons' Terrace, Hyde Park.

VICTORIA BRANCH:
HEAD OFFICE: 35, QUEEN-STREET, MELBOURNE.

NEW ZEALAND BRANCH:
HEAD OFFICE: GREY-STREET, WELLINGTON.

SOUTH AUSTRALIAN BRANCH:
HEAD OFFICE: 10, KING WILLIAM-STREET, ADELAIDE.

Agencies in all the Principal Towns throughout New South Wales, Victoria, Queensland, South Australia, New Zealand, and Tasmania.

The Society was Established in 1849, and has now achieved a position of Affluence and Stability unsurpassed in the history of Life Assurance Institutions at Home or Abroad.

The Accumulated and Invested Funds now exceed £1,151,100
The Annual Revenue exceeds £282,672

The Last Year's Income was Increased by £42,270 19s. 5d., resulting from the Issue of 2,926 Policies, Assuring £830,904; a rate of progress which entitles the Society to rank with the First-class Assurance Institutions of the United Kingdom.

The Fourth Quinquennial Report, showing the Society's State and Progress, Prospectuses, and Forms of Proposal, may be had, or will be sent, post free, on application to the Principal Office, or any of the Society's Agents.

ALEXANDER J. RALSTON, Secretary.

www.ingramcontent.com/pod-product-compliance
Lightning Source LLC
Chambersburg PA
CBHW021938160426
43195CB00011B/1131